Hope

THE KESWICK
YEAR BOOK **2020**

CHRISTOPHER ASH

MICHAEL REEVES

JOANNA JACKSON

RICO VILLANUEVA

Hope

MIKE CAIN

ANDY PRIME

AMY ORR-EWING

GRAHAM DANIELS

JEREMY McQUOID

First published 2021

British Library Cataloguing-in-Publication Data
A catalogue record for this book is available from the British Library.

ISBN: 978–1–78974–332–6
eBook ISBN: 978–1–78974–334–0

Set in Dante 12.5/16pt
Typeset in Great Britain by CRB Associates, Potterhanworth, Lincolnshire
Printed and bound in Great Britain by Ashford Colour Press Ltd, Gosport, Hampshire

Contents

Evening Celebrations

Introduction

The year 2020 was unprecedented for the Keswick Convention. A Convention with the theme 'Grateful' had been planned, speakers had been booked and preparations were in full swing when the Covid-19 pandemic struck the world. The trustees of Keswick Ministries decided, with a few months to go, to cancel the physical event in Keswick and to hold a five-day Convention online, Virtually Keswick Convention, with the theme 'Hope'.

New passages were chosen, new speakers were booked, new seminars were planned, a new kids and youth programme was devised, a new website was designed and there was a new method of delivery. Rather than speaking directly to a packed tent, contributors spoke to a camera. Some were filmed in their homes, but most of the programme was filmed inside the disused pencil factory building, currently in the midst of being refurbished as part of the Derwent Project. Much of the content is still available online, on the Keswick Convention YouTube channel.

The online Virtually Keswick Convention brought fresh opportunities. Some speakers and those serving on the mission field were filmed in their own contexts. And many more people from across the UK and the world could engage with the Convention, both those who had never been before and those who are unable to come to the Lake District.

'Hope' was chosen as the theme because, at a time of great uncertainty in the middle of a global pandemic, there is hope in Jesus Christ. Even in the midst of struggle, hardship, suffering and pain, we can, by the power of the Holy Spirit, be filled to overflowing with joy and peace from the God of hope (Romans 15:13).

A Christian does not pretend that things are good when they are not. We are willing to face the real and the raw. But we are not prisoners of the present moment. Our mood, our well-being and our identity are not defined by our circumstances or our situation. Rather, every Christian is shaped by looking back and looking forwards. We look back to Jesus' life, death, resurrection and ascension, and the pouring out of the Holy Spirit. But we don't just look back. We also look forward – eagerly – to the return and reign of Christ in a new heaven and a new earth, and the day when death is swallowed up in victory.

And this future is not a matter of wish-fulfilment or pious idealism. Rather, it is secured – held firm – by the sure and certain promises of God. So, we are not confined by what seems reasonable based on the present and its possibilities. No. We are shaped – even set free – by what is possible to the God of promise, the God of hope.

The 2020 Convention gave a chance for all who joined to face the real and the raw. It provided an opportunity for them to have their hope in Christ renewed, recalibrated and refocused by the Holy Spirit through the preaching of God's Word.

The following chapters provide a snapshot of the engaging preaching and teaching, rooted in the Word of God, that saw thousands of all ages inspired and equipped to love and live for Christ in his world. Young and old alike experienced fresh joy and peace as they trusted in Christ, knowing the power of the Holy Spirit as hope overflowed (Romans 15:13).

There are three Bible Readings by Christopher Ash on Psalms 2, 3 and 6. From these psalms, Christopher unpacks carefully, faithfully, insightfully and pastorally the hope we can have in Jesus Christ: hope because Jesus rules (Psalm 2); hope because Jesus was saved (Psalm 3); and hope because Jesus wept (Psalm 6).

There are all five sermons from the Evening Celebrations, each focusing on a different aspect of hope: Mike Cain on 'Why Hope? Grace!' (2 Thessalonians 2:13–17); Andy Prime on 'How Can I Hope? New Birth!' (1 Peter 1:3–5, 22–25); Amy Orr-Ewing on 'How Can I Hope? The Scriptures!' (Romans 15:1–13); Graham Daniels on 'Our Hope: The Appearing of Jesus Christ' (Titus 2:11–14);

and Jeremy McQuoid on 'Our Hope: The Glory of God!' (Romans 5:1–5).

Finally, there are three Seminars. The first, by Michael Reeves, looks from a fresh angle at 'Our Future Hope', unpacking the biblical hope of new heavens and a new earth, and how that hope can transform our lives now. The second, by Joanna Jackson, explores 'Hope and Grief', helping us to 'grieve in hope' and to know and give the comfort of Jesus in our grief. The third, by Rico Villanueva, 'Hope and Lament', shows us that there is room for our struggles in the presence of the Lord.

Alongside this Year Book, we would like to recommend to you two resources that we produced for 2020. The first is a new series of thematic thirty-day Food for the Journey devotionals. The first three of these devotionals are now available: *Joy, Pray* and *Persevere*. With them, you can read the Bible with experienced teachers from the Keswick Convention by your side. The second is the theme book for the original Convention, *Radical Gratitude: Recalibrating Your Heart in an Age of Entitlement* by Peter Maiden. Peter, a dear servant and friend of Keswick Ministries over many years, went to be with the Lord in July 2020, but not before he saw this powerful, honest and penetrating book in his hands. D. A. Carson wrote of it, 'In an age when whining has become a pandemic . . . Peter provides us with a profoundly biblical alternative.'[1]

The Lord alone knows the impact that the 2020 Convention will have. But we can be confident that when God's Word is spoken, by the power of his Spirit, lives are changed. As you read this book, it is our prayer that your hope in Christ will be renewed, so you will be filled with all joy and peace in believing, and be inspired and encouraged to love Christ and live for him in his world.

James Robson
Ministry Director
Keswick Ministries

Note

1. From an endorsement by D. A. Carson on p. i of Peter Maiden, *Radical Gratitude: Recalibrating Your Heart in an Age of Entitlement* (IVP, 2020).

The Bible Readings

Hope in Jesus
Psalms

Christopher Ash

Christopher Ash is Writer-in-Residence at Tyndale House, Cambridge, and is on the preaching team at St Andrew the Great. Christopher is a pastor, preacher and author. He has written several books on the Psalms: *Bible Delight* (on Psalm 119), *Teaching Psalms* (two volumes) and *Psalms for You*. He is working on a longer commentary about how we appropriate the psalms deeply in Christ. Christopher is married to Carolyn. They have been entrusted with three sons, a daughter and seven grandchildren.

Hope because Jesus Rules
(Psalm 2)

Do you want to be safe? Of course you do, and so do I. The strange thing, preaching to a camera, is that I don't know who you are, listening to this. But I know we are surrounded by many dangers. At the moment, the virus is in the headlines. But there are many more dangers – heart disease, cancers, dementia, accidents on the roads and in the home, bereavement, broken relationships, abuse, redundancy, and – in many parts of the world – war, terrorism and starvation. We live in a dangerous world, and you and I want to be safe.

Our theme for this Virtually Keswick week is hope: hope in a world of fear; hope in a society riven with anxiety.

I have chosen to speak from five consecutive psalms (Psalms 2–6). It's really good to read psalms in order; there are all sorts of links. In a way, they tell a story. Psalm 1 was expounded quite recently at Keswick. So, today, I'll begin with Psalm 2. Psalms 1 and 2 are the lighted gateposts at the entrance of the psalter; they shine their bright rays through the whole book.

Psalm 2 offers us hope because Jesus rules. There are three vivid scenes and then a conclusion.

Scene 1: one pointless riot (Psalm 2:1–3)

It begins with a scene that is stupid and yet frightening. 'Why' – the first word of the psalm – expresses bewilderment. 'What I am about to describe', says David, 'is absurd; it's pointless.' But it's frightening. 'Why do the nations' – all over the world, all through history – 'rage' in a restless commotion? It has the feel of a mob rioting. Think of the riot in Ephesus, so vividly described in Acts 19. The nations rage, shouting angrily. Or, to put it another way, 'the peoples plot' – the word for 'plot' is the same word used for 'meditates' in Psalm 1:2. They mutter, they chatter, they tweet, they post blogs, they speak on podcasts, they chat on chat shows, they murmur in gangs – and it is all 'in vain'. Those little words 'why' and 'in vain' in Psalm 2:1 signal, right at the start, that what we are about to see is all pointless.

But what is it that is pointless? Verse 2: 'the kings of the earth set themselves' – like marshalling forces for battle, taking their stand, determined, united – or, to put it another way, 'the rulers take counsel together', setting the assumptions for their societies – what people are allowed to believe and how they are expected to behave. Who are these 'kings of the earth . . . rulers'? They are powerful people. They certainly include presidents and prime ministers: the President of China, listen to this; the President of the USA, listen to this; the President of Russia, listen to this; the Prime Minister of the UK, listen to this. They are anyone with influence – celebrities, bloggers, managers, head teachers and parents in families; actually, they are anyone who makes a difference in the world. We may think that we are not kings or rulers but, so long as we are alive, we make a difference to those around us – what we say or don't say, whether we smile or frown, what we choose to do – so we need to listen, too.

It's worth thinking about the power we have. I suspect that, sometimes, we don't realize the power we have. We've been made aware recently of the privilege that comes to some of us simply because of the colour of our skin, and the prejudice experienced by others for the same reason. There is power that comes from money; those of us who have money can use our money to increase our influence and to build our empires. Power can come from a privileged education or from being well connected. A pastor may enjoy great powers of spiritual influence and leadership. All these powers can be abused, misused and turned to our own benefit. So, as we look at this scene, let's see ourselves there.

It's a picture of a riotous crowd, a tumultuous scene, and it occurs all over the world. This riot is 'against the

LORD [the covenant God of the Bible] and against his Anointed' (the Hebrew word from which we get 'messiah'), the anointed king(s), David and his heirs. This anointed one is so intimately linked to the Lord that hostility to him is enmity to God ('Whoever hates me hates my Father also' as a later Anointed One will say in John 15:23.)

What do they say? Listen to them shout: 'Let us burst their bonds apart and cast away their cords from us' (Psalm 2:3). It's a great worldwide freedom movement: 'We do not want to be ruled by the God of the Bible and certainly not by his Messiah, his Anointed King. No, no, no! We want to make our own decisions, thank you very much.'

Normally, when there are lots of powerful people, they disagree with one another; they vie for power. And they do. But there is one thing that unites them: 'We do not want God's man to rule over us! We are agreed on that. If we can get rid of God's King, we can carry on fighting one another as usual.'

We live in a world that is united in a pointless but terrifying rebellion. And, by nature, we are part of that world. Every baby, each boy and girl, teenager, young person, middle-aged man or woman, and older person is a part of that world, until and unless we bow the knee to Jesus. We disagree about many things but we are united in this: we want the right to make our own decisions. 'I want to be true to myself,' we each say.

It's really important to grasp that each of us is a part of this riot. We join in this commotion. When I was at school in the late 1960s and early 1970s there were lots of (sometimes violent) demonstrations against the Vietnam War. A boy in my year played truant from school one day. He went to London and got caught up in one of the demonstrations. When his teacher accused him the next day, he denied it. But – this was the problem – he had been on television on the evening news, clearly visible! He was guilty.

If the news report of this riot – the one pointless riot that is human history – were shown, you would be there and so would I.

This riot is stupid; it's 'in vain' but it's frightening if you're in the middle of it. And we are. Even Herod and Pontius Pilate, who had been enemies, became friends when Jesus came over their horizon (Luke 23:12). How terrifying when Herod and Pontius Pilate, along with the Roman imperial power and leaders of the Jews, gathered together against the Messiah, plotting, raging with fury and finally succeeding – or so it seemed – in having him crucified. In Acts 4:25–28, that's what we read. And it goes on and on: the apostles quote from these verses when they themselves are persecuted; thus it will be to the very end. These verses are echoed again in Revelation 19:19, 'the kings of the earth with their armies gathered to make war against him who is sitting on the horse [Jesus Christ] and against his army', his people.

We live in a dangerous, tumultuous world that riots against the rule of God and his Messiah. A world in which we cannot feel safe; a world in which, by nature, we contribute to the chaos. We will come back to that world at the end (Psalm 2:10–12). But, for now, the drama shifts to a very different scene.

Scene 2: one perfect King (Psalm2:4–6)

If scene 1 is stupid, chaotic, riotous and frightening, scene 2 is also frightening, but in a very different way. The camera pans away from the riot and now there is a surprise. We might expect a phalanx of divine riot police ready to impose order; instead, we see one laughing!

We are taken up above the riot to 'the heavens', God's 'place' (not a location in our space–time universe but above it all, unreachable, untouchable), which cannot be threatened by these angry voices. We can riot as much as we like down here but we cannot disturb up there. 'He who sits in the heavens laughs [at the absurdity of it all]; the Lord holds them in derision' (verse 4). As they so often do, the Scriptures use anthropomorphic (human-like) language to help us understand the demeanour of the unchanged and unchangeable God. It is as though he laughs at the sheer stupidity of it. Thomas Aquinas compared opposing God to a little boy, a toddler, seriously trying to beat a huge man in a fight: the huge man laughs; he's not frightened. Luther says it's like someone trying to knock down a stone tower with a few twigs.

But God doesn't just laugh; he speaks. 'Then he will speak to them in his wrath [his hot, settled, unchangeable righteous anger], and terrify them in his fury' (verse 5).

God (if we may put it this way) does not think our rebellion is funny. It is absurd, but it is not ha-ha funny. In the heart of God there is a hot, settled anger at men and women determined to make their own independent decisions, to live in God's world without God, to say of his King, 'We do not want this man to reign over us' (Luke 19:14).

And he says in verse 6, 'As for me' – it's emphatic: 'This is what I have done, and you cannot change it' – 'I have set my King on Zion, my holy hill.' Zion was the city of David that became a focus for the covenant of God with David that echoes through so much of the Old Testament: 'I have set my King there, my Anointed One, my Messiah-King, my Christ.'

Now we might object that this is just exchanging one bad government for another. Think of the French, Russian or even the English Revolution, where one bad government was exchanged for another. It may seem as if God is saying, 'This is my chosen ruler and you'll just have to lump it.' One of the big objections to religion is that it is divisive, with some claiming, 'We have the ruler and you don't.' People see it as abusive, the idea that God votes to sweep away human freedom. Religion can be an ugly thing.

But then we forget Psalm 1. Psalms 1 and 2 are closely linked in several ways. Psalm 1 says that when someone delights in the law of the Lord and walks that way, he will prosper in all that he does. There is a law in Deuteronomy 17 which says that when you have a king, he has to be a Psalm 1 man; he has to love and live by the law of

God. David was only partially a Psalm 1 man; scandalously, he abused his power to trash the seventh commandment with Bathsheba and the sixth by having her husband killed. A few of his successors – think of Hezekiah and Josiah – were approximately Psalm 1 men; most were emphatically not – think of Manasseh!

All through Old Testament history, the people were waiting for a Psalm 2 king who would be a Psalm 1 man. They went on waiting during and after the exile in Babylon (when there wasn't even a king in David's line at all) because they believed that, one day, there would be a 'son of David' who would inherit Psalm 2 because he fulfilled Psalm 1. They had to wait many years, but they did not wait in vain. And when he came, the rule he heralded was a perfect rule.

Now the camera returns to earth. And we hear the Anointed (Psalm 2:2), the Messiah, the King (verse 6) speak.

Scene 3: one praying Son (Psalm 2:7–9)

There is going to be a man on the throne of the world; a second Adam. We see him again in Psalm 8, waiting to rule the world to come. We hear him here. We find he is the Son of God and he prays. Hear the voice of the Anointed King: 'I will tell of the decree' (Psalm 2:7) – this is something sure, unchangeable; it is the solid truth we need to know. 'The LORD [the covenant God] said to me, "You are my Son"'. Pause there. The tap root of the covenant is a relationship between the Father and the Son. All the blessings of the new covenant, as of the old, come from this relationship in eternity.

All over the ancient world, kings would claim to be sons of God. The king has access to God. The king carries the authority of God. The same promise of sonship was given to David in 2 Samuel 7:14: 'I will be to [him and his descendants] a father, and he shall be to me a son.' The people of Israel had been called the son of God at the time of the exodus: 'Israel is my firstborn son' (Exodus 4:22) and in the Prophets (Hosea 11:1: 'out of Egypt I called my son'). The king embodied that as the covenant head of the people: 'You are my Son.'

But there is something more going on here, as we shall see when we look at the prayer and the promise. 'Ask of me' (Psalm 2:8) – the greatest privilege of the Son is to ask, to pray and to have access to God the Father. The Father doesn't just give the Son what he promises. He tells the Son that he can ask for it. There's a deep relationship at work here. The Father loves the Son; the Son loves the Father; the Father knows what the Son needs before he asks, but he wants him to ask.

And what a promise! 'I will make the nations your heritage' (verse 8). Those rebellious nations of verse 1, raging for 'freedom', will be his 'heritage', his Promised Land and (if we are in any doubt about the extent of the promise) 'the ends of the earth [his] possession'. No limit smaller than the whole world. It will all be his to rule. This is the promise to Abraham to inherit the earth as Paul expresses it in Romans 4:13. This is the calling of the second Adam, to subdue the earth.

'You shall break them' – the Greek Old Testament says 'rule them' or 'shepherd them'; the New Testament adds 'with a rod' (Revelation 2:27; 12:5; 19:15), the same word used for a shepherd's staff in Psalm 23. It is an irresistible rod 'of iron'. And the Son will 'dash them in pieces like a potter's vessel'. The second line almost certainly means a judgment of destruction, a piece of pottery smashed to smithereens. The first line probably at least hints at something more hopeful, a shepherding rule that breaks in order to mend; a gospel rule that breaks a hard heart, that takes down obstacles to the rule of Christ. But whether it is destruction or a pastoral breaking and remaking, it is an irresistible rule.

Three times at least the book of Revelation echoes this. For example, in Revelation 12:5, the symbolic woman 'gave birth to a male child, one who is to rule all the nations with a rod of iron'. And, again, in Revelation 19:15, from the mouth of the conquering rider on the white horse 'comes a sharp sword with which to strike down the nations, and he will rule them with a rod of iron'. So, there's a promise of worldwide irresistible rule; the kingdom of David in the Old Testament was – as Calvin put it – 'merely a shadow' of that of the Christ to come.

Here is the Anointed (the Messiah, Psalm 2:2), the King (verse 6), the Son of God (verse 7) (this is the only Old Testament scripture with those three great titles in it), who is a second Adam to govern the whole world as it ought to be governed, to bring the order of God's law into a disordered world, to bring hope in a world of danger.

John the Baptist, in the middle of a busy day of baptisms, baptizes his cousin Jesus from Nazareth, and the voice from heaven says, 'This – this! – is my Son. You are my Son, with you I am well pleased' (see Matthew 3:17). At last, the Psalm 2 Son who is the pleasing Psalm 1 man! We listen with Peter, James and John on the Mount of Transfiguration, and we hear that voice again, 'This is my beloved Son . . . listen to him' (Matthew 17:5).

But what about '*today* I have begotten you' (Psalm 2:7, my emphasis)? It is all very well for David to become the son of God, or his heirs when they were anointed. But for Jesus? It's an ancient heresy that Jesus was not the eternal Son of God but became the Son of God, perhaps at his baptism or his resurrection. But he is the eternal Son of God. Some of the older writers, including Augustine and Luther, suggested that 'today' must stand outside of time – the unending 'today' of eternity. But the New Testament suggests that 'today' here means the resurrection, ascension and heavenly session of Jesus.

Paul in Acts 13:32–33 says, 'What God promised . . . this he has fulfilled to us . . . by raising Jesus, as also it is written in the second Psalm, "You are my Son, today I have begotten you."' At the beginning of Paul's letter to the Romans, he talks about Jesus' being declared or appointed Son of God in power by his resurrection (Romans 1:4). So, the New Testament indicates that, at his resurrection, Jesus is made Son of God in power. He has been Son of God from all eternity (the Father has loved him as Son; the Son has loved him from all eternity) and now, in resurrection, he is appointed Son of God in power: he's given the name that is above every name (Philippians 2:9–11); he's given all authority over heaven and earth; he can rule the world (Matthew 28:18). All this happens in this age through the gospel of Jesus the Lord. As that gospel is preached all over the world, one after another bows the knee to Jesus. 'Ask of me, and I will make the nations your heritage': Jesus asks – the answer is the worldwide missionary ministry of the gospel of Christ.

And so what? A great decision and a safe place (Psalm 2:10–12)

'Now therefore, O kings,' says David in Psalm 2:10; the voice is one we hear in Proverbs, of a parent to a child: 'Now listen carefully to me, little one.' Only these are kings! Is this not impertinent? Well, it would be, except for the one who says it.

> Now therefore, O kings [you who want to live your lives making your own decisions, unfettered by God's law, untied to God's Messiah – now that you have heard the voice from heaven (verse 6) and the Messiah telling of the decree (the relationship, the prayer, the promise (verses 7–9)), now that you have heard all this], be wise; be warned, O rulers of the earth. [Don't be stupid.] . . .

> Serve the LORD [the covenant God of the Bible] with fear
> [reverent fear] and rejoice with trembling.
>
> (verses 10–11)

That's a strange combination! Rejoice because his government is good, but with trembling because you will never be more than his servants. God the Father is infinitely great: tremble before him. God the Son is matchless in power: tremble before him. God the Holy Spirit is awesome in holiness: tremble before him. Tremble before the Triune God. And rejoice as you tremble.

'Kiss the Son' – that is, with a kiss of homage, a bit like our custom of kissing the ring of a sovereign as a sign of pledging loyalty. 'Kiss the Son, lest he be angry, and you perish in the way' – an echo of the end of Psalm 1, 'the way of the wicked will perish' – 'for his wrath is quickly kindled' (verse 12). God is not hot-tempered, for God is 'slow to anger' (see Exodus 34:6). But when he does act, he will do it quickly and there will be no escape. So 'kiss the Son' now, while there is time, while God is patient. His patience is to lead you to repentance. Repent today. Repent again each day.

There is no room for pride or self-righteousness. Think about where you have power. You may be a pastor: your church is not your empire; it belongs to Jesus. You may head a department or be a manager at work: your department is not your empire; it belongs to Jesus. If you love your importance, you will abuse it, treating people as being there for you. No, you are there to serve Jesus and serve people for Jesus' sake. You may be a parent: your family is not your empire; it belongs to Jesus. You may be a husband, a wife, an unmarried person or someone very frail through sickness: you make a difference, whether by throwing your weight around or treating others as more important than yourself, by grumbling or thankfulness. Whoever you are, let this psalm call you to bow the knee to Jesus afresh.

And then take comfort. The psalm ends, as Psalm 1 begins, by declaring a blessing: 'Blessed are all who take refuge in him' (Psalm 2:12). There is a safe place, but only one. You and I cannot find refuge away from the Messiah, the King, the Son of God, for his rule extends to the ends of the earth. But we can and must find refuge in him. That is the place of blessing.

In Revelation 2:26–27, the risen Jesus astonishingly applies the promise of worldwide rule, not only to himself, but to the believer:

> The one who conquers [that is, goes on believing and bearing testimony to Jesus to the end] and who keeps my works until the end, to him I will give authority over the nations, and he will rule them with a rod of iron, as when earthen pots are broken in pieces, even as I myself have received authority from my Father.

How extraordinary! When you look at the most unimpressive believer, he or she is not at all a king or ruler or imposing person in the eyes of the world. Rather, she trusts in Jesus; he prays; she bears testimony. 'This one', says Jesus, 'will share in the government of the age to come!' And the promise of Psalm 2 comes to you and to me, in Jesus. We have hope because Jesus rules. Not just hope that we will survive but also hope that we will share his government of the new creation.

You want a safe place; so do I. There is only one. There is hope because Jesus rules. May God bring this home to our hearts. Amen.

Hope because Jesus Was Saved
(Psalm 3)

Psalm 3 is about living under pressure. Many of you know what it is to be under pressure. Plenty of you are under pressure right now. You feel squeezed. In your workplace, neighbourhood or family, you know how hard it is to live for Christ. Some of you have been locked down with a family who do not understand your faith in Christ; some may be hostile. Others, especially those active in Christian service, may feel the pressure of people: so many people, with all their problems. Or you may just be feeling the pressure of time and tasks: so much to do, so little time and energy to do it. For much of the worldwide church of Christ, it is much grittier than that – a simple, direct, threatening pressure of persistent persecution.

Yesterday, in Psalm 2, we watched spellbound as God in heaven laughs at the absurd riot against God and his Anointed, his Messiah, his Christ. We watched that Son, that Christ, that King promise that he will rule the world. It was a great start to the Psalms. But how will that world domination happen? The answer is . . . through deep suffering.

From Psalm 3, we are plunged into the struggles of that Anointed King, from the mountain peak of promise to the depths of suffering. We fast forward to the terrible time when David flees Jerusalem because his son Absalom wants his throne (2 Samuel 15 – 18). In some ways, David deserved that. It is the entailment of his ugly sin with Bathsheba and against Uriah her husband (2 Samuel 11). But (unlike King Saul who never repented) David has repented and been forgiven. He is still the anointed king. Absalom is wrong to rebel. Just as the promise to David in Psalm 2 finds its fulfilment as the promise to Jesus, so the struggles of David in Psalm 3 foreshadow the struggles of David's greater Son. And then they overflow to all Christ's people.

I want to say four things to you, one from each pair of verses, as we learn to make Psalm 3 part of our prayer lives. The first, in verses 1–2, is very sobering.

Expect this pressure, in Christ (Psalm 3:1–2)

'O LORD [the covenant name of the Lord who has made promises to his King], how many are my foes!' 'Foes' is a word that speaks of pressure. Can you see the crescendo? The foes were there but somehow static, but now 'many are rising against' the King. His foes are rising up in rebellion, which is exactly what Absalom had done. David knew that. Years later, King Hezekiah had the same experience when surrounded by the Assyrian armies – so many, there they all were, row after row of warriors, line after line, file after file, all around (2 Kings 18 – 19).

In the end, Jesus went through that: this is the rebellion at the start of Psalm 2. Not everybody was involved, but almost all the powerful people – the chief priests, the Sadducees, the popular Pharisees (who would be the social media stars and YouTubers of today), the Romans, Herod – were against him. He walked this earth surrounded by those who hated him, who were plotting to kill him and rising up against him. You can feel the pressure.

But the climax comes in Psalm 3:2. Here is the worst thing they do: it's not just that they're there (line 1); it's not just that they rise up (line 2); they say something! 'Many are saying of my soul [of the core of my being]' – they are doing something that no sword or spear can do; they are wielding a weapon that reaches to the core of the psalmist's spirit. They say, 'There is no salvation for him in God.' God won't help him.

And then that little word *Selah*. We don't know what it means but it probably means something like a pause for reflection, perhaps a musical pause. Even if it doesn't, it won't do any harm to follow Luther's suggestion of pausing to meditate. So, let's pause. The worst thing they do is not to wield their swords or spears, it is to say something to us: 'God isn't going to help you. Not only is the experience terrible; there is no hope. This lockdown will never end. You will be squeezed and squeezed until you are crushed.'

They said, 'God isn't going to help you,' to David as he crossed the brook Kidron and climbed the Mount of Olives. They said that in mockery to Jesus, who had also crossed the brook Kidron and climbed the Mount of Olives to Gethsemane. The next day they jeered: 'He trusts in God; let God deliver him now, if he desires him. For he said, "I am the Son of God"' (Matthew 27:43). 'But', they are thinking, 'we don't think he will! God isn't going to help *him*!' You wonder how that mockery went to the very soul of Jesus.

Jesus had spoken with confidence: 'I have authority to lay it [my life] down, and I have authority to take it up again. This charge I have received from my Father' (John 10:18). His Father had given him this authority but now he is 'made sin' for us (2 Corinthians 5:21). As the crushing burden and the awful darkness close in on him, he hears these voices: 'God's not going to help *you*! You are fooling yourself if you think you are the Son of God.' Was it true? Is it true? Can he who has been made sin really continue to entrust himself to the one who judges justly? It's a terrible jibe. And it hurts so much.

You and I need to expect that the whole church of Christ will be constricted by a sceptical world, persecuted all over the globe, and squeezed by the world, the flesh and the devil. All around, there will be many who think that God isn't going to help *us*. If we live in India, the Hindu majority do not think God will help us, because they believe the gods and goddesses to be those of Hinduism:

'Don't expect god to help *you*,' they think. 'You are following the wrong god.' If we live in Japan, those who follow Shinto do not think God will help us, because (they believe) we need to worship the gods and spirits of the Shinto shrines. If we live in an Islamic country, most people do not think God will help *us*, for (they believe) we are following the wrong god. If we belong to a Buddhist culture, we can't expect a non-existent god to help us, for we are following the wrong path. If we inhabit a secular Western culture, we shouldn't expect our non-existent god to help us. 'No,' they think, 'that might have brought some comfort to your parents or grandparents, but it's not true.'

This is the normal experience of the church of Christ. Expect it. That voice saying – all over the world – 'there is no salvation in God for *you*' is deeply unsettling. Children growing up in a Christian home begin to hear it at an early age. The raised eyebrow of surprise when they begin to talk innocently about Jesus; the curled lip of the sneer at secondary school; the cold shoulder of exclusion if they are too up front about following Jesus at college. I think of a friend of mine who acted honourably and was vilified for it; and of two other friends falsely accused of misbehaviour and having to endure a long process to clear their names, with no assurance of justice.

Of course, there's a particular twist to this that comes from our sin. We hear this terrible whisper: 'There's no salvation for *you* from God. Perhaps for others but not for *you*.' The devil uses our sin at times like this. As Ayguan, a medieval writer puts it:

The craft of the devil is often displayed in representing a sin to which we are tempted as trifling [huh! That's not a big thing to do; that doesn't matter]; after we have committed it, as so great that there is no help for us in our God [What! You did *that*!][1]

'How can God be expected to help *you*, you who said that, you who acted out on that lust, you who trampled on a work colleague, you who denied Christ.' And the memory of a sin grows and haunts our nightmares. 'Oh, you deserve this pressure, whatever it is. Don't expect God to help *you*.' This taunt is more deadly to David than arrows, more painful to Jesus than the nails and more grievous to his followers than martyrdom. Don't be surprised. Expect this pressure, in Christ. But don't stop with Psalm 3:2.

Claim the promises, in Christ (Psalm 3:3–4)

'But you, O LORD' is emphatic; his foes are speaking about him but he is not speaking to them; he prays. They jeer at him; he cries to God. David lays claim to four kingly privileges. Each of these belongs supremely to Jesus Christ and each one is ours in Christ.

Safety
First, safety: 'you . . . are a shield about me' (verse 3); you protect me from the flaming arrows of the evil one. We talk about 'shielding' from the coronavirus, but here is an even better shielding! God says, 'I have set my King on

Zion, my holy hill' (Psalm 2:6). It is laughable to try to unseat him. 'Don't even think about it,' God says. 'I am a shield around him.' That was the confidence of David; it became the assurance of Jesus: 'Father, you are a shield about me. They cannot do to me one millimetre beyond what you decree. When I drink the cup of God's wrath, I do not drink it because my enemies force me to; I drink it because my Father gives it to me, that I may die for sinners and save a people. You are a shield about me even then, in some strange, deep, wonderful way.'

Then Jesus says to us,

[If my Father is your heavenly Father,] you will be delivered up even by parents and brothers and relatives and friends, and some of you they will put to death. You will be hated by all for my name's sake. But not a hair of your head will perish.
(Luke 21:16–18)

In Christ, our heavenly Father is a shield about us. Claim the promise, in Christ.

Dignity
Second, dignity: 'you are my glory' (Psalm 3:3). This is the dignity given to the king. Wherever this word is used of a human being in the Psalms, it is applied to the king in David's line. 'You give me great dignity, honour and glory,' the psalmist is saying. 'People may mock, spit, insult and dishonour, but you are my glory and my dignity, and that

can't be destroyed.' David trusted that promise. Jesus trusted that promise: 'Father, you are my glory; my kingly dignity is safe with you.' Jesus' glory was veiled, dishonoured, abused and vilified, but the Father guarantees his kingly glory. One day, every man or woman who has ever lived will see the kingly glory of Jesus and bow the knee to him.

If you belong to Jesus Christ, you too 'are being transformed . . . from one degree of glory to another' (2 Corinthians 3:18). The whole creation waits on tiptoe for the sons of God to be revealed (see Romans 8:19). One day every man and every woman who belongs to Jesus will come into the inheritance that a son would have expected in the ancient world. You look around now; those who belong to Jesus are usually unimpressive. They are not usually in the glamour magazines or commemorated on memorials. They are not the people with face recognition all over the world. One day, the world will gaze in wonder at the dignity given to each man and woman in Christ. Safety. Dignity. Claim the promises, in Christ.

Victory

Third, victory: 'you are the lifter of my head' (Psalm 3:3). When David fled Absalom, he went up the Mount of Olives, 'weeping as he went, barefoot and with his head covered' in disgrace (2 Samuel 15:30). No doubt his head was also bowed with sadness, in apparent defeat. He was a loser, wasn't he? And yet, in his prayers, he could say,

'You, the covenant Lord, you are the lifter of my head. One day, I will rule again.'

We may imagine the Lord Jesus saying, as he prayed this psalm in his earthly life, 'Father, you are the lifter of my head. One day, I will rule the world. It doesn't feel like it now; it doesn't much look like it, but it's true. You said I could ask for that. I have asked; I do ask; and I believe you are the lifter of my head. I entrust myself to you.'

If you belong to Jesus, this too is yours in him. 'Father, I belong to Jesus your Son, my King. And so, in him, you are the lifter, even of my sorrowful head.' Remember that great phrase in the letters to the churches in Revelation, 'the one who conquers' (see Revelation 2 and 3)? This is the one who goes on following Jesus to the end. This man, this woman and this youngster will conquer; by their simple persevering faith, they overcome the world. As 1 John 5:4 says, 'This is the victory that has overcome the world – our faith.' God will lift your head in victory and you will share with Jesus the government of the age to come! Claim the promises, in Christ.

Safety, dignity, victory. And, fourth, the power of prayer.

Prayer

'I cried aloud to the Lord, and he answered me from his holy hill' (Psalm 3:4). This is the 'holy hill' of Psalm 2:6, the place of the promise, of the covenant with the King, the Messiah, the Son of God.

'You say there is no rescue for me from God? But I have the privilege of prayer. My Father said to me, "Ask of me"

(Psalm 2:8). I do ask and I know he will answer.' This was the privilege of David in shadow; it was the birthright of Jesus in fullness. 'Father . . . I knew that you always hear me,' says Jesus at the tomb of Lazarus in John 11:41–42. And in the name of Jesus – but only in the name of Jesus – you and I may know the power of prayer. Down the centuries, believer after believer has testified, 'I cried aloud to the Lord and he answered me' in Jesus' name.

At the end of Psalm 3:4 there's the *Selah* again. So, let's pause. When you feel the pressure in Christ – and you will – claim the promises. These are the promises given to Jesus our King. And, if you belong to Jesus, they are all yours in him: safety, dignity, victory and prayer. But there is more. Not only do we claim the promises, we enjoy them.

Enjoy the promises, in Christ (Psalm 3:5–6)

> I lay down and slept;
>   I woke again, for the LORD sustained me.
> I will not be afraid . . .

This is extraordinary. It is clear from verse 6 that nothing has changed. If anything, it has got worse. In verses 1 and 2, there were 'many . . . many . . . many'; now there are 'many thousands' – an incalculable multitude. They have 'set themselves' in battle array and they are 'all around', on every side. David is in very great danger.

Yet, he lies down and sleeps. Not just once but habitually. You can translate it as 'I lie down and sleep, night after night, and I wake again. That's what I do.' But it's what you *don't do* when your life is in danger! You know as well as I do that pressure destroys sleep; worry messes with sleep; fear disrupts sleep. And yet he sleeps. He does not sleep just because he is tired. He sleeps because he believes and enjoys the promises of verses 3 and 4: 'God has anointed me his King, his Messiah, his Son and so I can sleep; and I know that I will wake up.'

David did that in some measure, and it was wonderful. But supremely Jesus did that: watched by enemies, pursued by powerful foes, he slept. Night after night, he lay down and slept. Morning by morning, he awoke. He slept on a boat tossed by the wild storm of all the forces of hell seeking to destroy him, for he trusted his Father's covenant love. He enjoyed the promises.

The promises of God are a wonderful pillow! As one old writer expressed it:

> Truly it must be a soft pillow indeed that could make him [David] forget his danger, who then had such a disloyal army at his back hunting of him; yea, so transcendent is the influence of this peace, that it can make the creature lie down as cheerfully to sleep in the grave, as on the softest bed.[2]

In some measure, you and I can enter into this. I know in my own experience that sleep is a strange thing, that there are many reasons why sleep is disturbed. There were times when the Lord Jesus spent all night in prayer. This is not talking about an easy life. The apostle Paul had sleepless nights and so will we. But the principle is this: when God makes promises that are ours in Christ, we are free, we are encouraged, we are stirred to enjoy them. When we do sleep, we do so knowing we will wake because Father God will sustain us. We enjoy our safety.

You may say, 'Sometimes people die in their sleep. What about that?' Once or twice in the Old Testament, waking from sleep is a picture of resurrection. Jesus used this language of Jairus' daughter in Mark 5:39: 'The child is not dead but sleeping.' People laughed at him for she was dead. But Jesus stands by her bed and says to her, 'Little girl, it's time to get up now.' And she gets up. About Lazarus, Jesus says, 'Our friend Lazarus has fallen asleep, but I go to awaken him' (John 11:11). The disciples thought that he meant Lazarus was just resting. But Jesus states clearly that Lazarus had died and he was going to wake him up. 'We do not want you to be uninformed . . . about those who are asleep,' writes Paul in 1 Thessalonians 4:13.

So, from the earliest Christian days, Psalm 3:5 has been understood to hint at a deeper truth. Not only does the King – not only do we – fall asleep and wake again and again, because the Lord sustains us, but even more, on that day when you and I fall asleep in death, we may do so with peace of heart, knowing we shall wake, as Jesus woke on his resurrection morning. We need not be afraid of all the hosts of hell for we fall asleep in Jesus. And just as he fell asleep and woke, so we will wake on resurrection morning.

Sometimes, in a country churchyard, you see on a gravestone 'Fell Asleep' and then a date or – better still –

'Fell Asleep in Jesus'. That brings a lump to my throat. You see a weeping family around the grave, lowering the coffin into the ground, watered by their tears. And yet, as they do, they know they are bidding their loved one a kind of long goodnight, as they sleep in Jesus.

Some years ago, my wife Carolyn and I were walking around Westminster Abbey, looking at the inscriptions in Poet's Corner. Some were deeply depressing, such as those of Oscar Wilde and other ungodly unbelievers. And then we came across this: 'Heare Lyes (Expecting the Second Comminge of our Saviour Christ) the body of Edmund Spencer (*sic*)' (the sixteenth-century Protestant poet). I wanted to shout 'Hallelujah!' One at least (in that often godless corner of the Abbey), asleep in Jesus, waiting for that great day.

'Look at Jesus,' says an old writer:

Behold the Son of David, composing himself to his rest upon the cross . . . and commending his spirit into the Father's hands, in full confidence of joyful resurrection. Behold this, O Christian: let faith teach thee how to sleep and how to die [remembering] the same God watches over thee, in thy bed and in thy grave.[3]

Truly that is a soft pillow indeed! Expect this pressure, in Christ. Claim these promises, in Christ – safety, dignity, victory, prayer. Enjoy these promises, in Christ – you can sleep knowing you will wake. And lastly . . .

Look forward to the victory, in Christ (Psalm 3:7–8)

'Arise, O LORD!' (verse 7). That's the prayer that they used to say in the Old Testament when the ark of the covenant went out with the people to lead them in their battles (Numbers 10). 'Arise, O Lord! Save me,' says the King. That's exactly what the mockers say that God won't do: 'there is no salvation for him in God' (Psalm 3:2). The King goes on, '[But you will save,] for you strike all my enemies on the cheek' – in their defeat and disgrace, a slap on the cheek. 'You break the teeth of the wicked' – they are like wild beasts, and you break their teeth so they can't tear their prey. Their words – 'there is no salvation for him in God' – don't sound so good with their teeth broken!

Jesus prayed, 'Arise, my Father! Save me, O my God!' And the Father did arise. He gave to Jesus 'the name that is above every name, so that at the name of Jesus every knee should bow' (Philippians 2:9–10). That cry, 'Arise, O LORD!' becomes for us the cry, 'Come, Lord Jesus!'

This is an intensely personal psalm by David the king, anticipating Jesus the King. The big question of the psalm is whether God will save the King (Psalm 3:2). So, look at verse 8: 'Salvation belongs to the LORD,' that is, he will save the King; he does save Jesus in resurrection. Therefore 'your blessing [will] be on your people!' Because the King is saved, all the blessings of the King overflow to the King's people. *Selah* – think about it.

Andrew Bonar, a nineteenth-century Scottish writer, says that 'when waves of sorrow and calamity are dashing over the ship of the Church', we may use this psalm. And when we do, we remember how Jesus once used it:

> My Head [Jesus, our covenant head] once used this Psalm; and while I use its strains, his human heart will recall the day of his humiliation, when he himself was comforted thereby . . . A believer can take up every clause, and sing it all in sympathy with his Head; hated by the same world that hated him; loved and kept by the same Father that lifted up his head; heard and answered and sustained as he was, and entering with him on final victory in the latter day.'[4]

Praise God! There is hope because Jesus was saved! There is hope because Jesus is the Saviour! Expect the pressure with him. Claim the promises with him. Enjoy the promises with him. Look forward to the victory in him.

Notes

1. J. S. Exell, *The Biblical Illustrator*, vol. 4 (Delmarva Publications, 2015).
2. William Gurnall, quoted in C. H. Spurgeon, *A Treasury of David: Vol. 1, Psalms I to XXVI* (Passmore and Alabaster, 1870), p. 30.
3. Matthew Henry, *Matthew Henry's Concise Commentary on the Whole Bible* (Thomas Nelson, 2003), p. 456.
4. Andrew Bonar, *Christ and His Church in the Book of Psalms* (Scholarly Publishing Office, 2005), pp. 10–11.

Hope because Jesus Wept
(Psalm 6)

I have been thinking recently about the sadness of sin; the sheer depth of sorrow that sin brings into the world. Maybe it's the coronavirus, the lockdown, the race riots; maybe it's just because I'm getting older. But many of you watching this will have on your hearts dear ones struggling with debilitating illness, life-threatening sickness, the dull pain of broken marriages, the tears of the childless, the weeping of the bereaved, the aching emptiness of those left behind by a suicide, the razor-sharp sword of a false accusation or the fearful tears of a breakdown. Sometimes as you pray, and all these griefs crowd in on you, you weep. If that is you – and it is certainly me – Psalm 6 will bring you hope because Jesus wept. This psalm will take you by the hand and bring you to a place of confidence and even joy in the midst of tears.

There are all sorts of links with Psalms 1 – 5: Psalm 6 is headed 'To the choirmaster', like Psalms 4 and 5. The

Sheminith may have been a tune; we don't know. Again, it's a psalm of David. And yet it feels different. It feels sad. It is sad – at least until the end. But it's a sadness that leads to gladness. So, come with me into what has traditionally been known as the first of the seven penitential psalms. It has been said that the Psalms give us a window into the human soul of Jesus. I think that's true. The Gospels give us occasional glimpses into how he feels – sorrow, indignation, anger, confidence, joy – but not very often do we see into the inner life of the Lord Jesus, the eternal Son of God taking on our full humanity in every facet of his being: his thinking, his emotions, his body, his sorrows. The Psalms most wonderfully throw open the shutters that we may enter, gaze and wonder at the soul of our Saviour.

Psalm 6 is an extraordinarily intense psalm. It has two loud echoes in the New Testament. The first is when the Lord Jesus says, in the shadow of the cross, 'Now is my soul troubled' (John 12:27). He echoes the words from verse 3 of this psalm: 'My soul also is greatly troubled.' Psalm 6 opens a window on to the troubled soul of Jesus. That's one echo. We'll come to the other echo later (see p. 50) because it is quite a surprise. I'm going to look at the psalm in three parts.

Feel the weight of God's wrath, as Jesus did (Psalm 6:1–3)

We'll start with verses 1–3. I want to encourage you, as I encourage myself, to feel the weight of God's wrath, as

Jesus felt it. We don't know what was going on in David's life when he wrote this. At the end of verse 7, he talks about 'foes', and we have met those enemies in almost all his psalms so far. But we don't know exactly what was happening. We do know that he felt himself to be under the anger of God: 'O Lord, rebuke me not in your anger, nor discipline me in your wrath' (verse 1).

Both those words, 'anger' and 'wrath', are used in Deuteronomy 29 about the destruction of Sodom and Gomorrah. They are hot words, strong words. I have been working with Steve Midgley on a book about anger and, when I read through the Bible, I found that most of the teaching on anger is about the wrath of God. That's what this psalm is about.

David feels himself to be under that wrath, and he's seen what happens when that righteous anger breaks out. In 2 Samuel 6, Uzzah casually reaches out and touches the ark of the covenant; the hot anger of God breaks out and he dies. David knows to take the holy anger of God seriously.

So, let me ask a question: how do you respond when something goes wrong? It may be a trivial thing – getting caught in a traffic jam or a washing machine breaking down. It may be very serious – bullying in the workplace, a life-threatening illness, the break-up of a marriage, the onset of dementia or the death of someone very dear. Those of you watching this will go through all these things and more. But how do you respond?

Sometimes I grumble – I complain about the government, about the person who has wronged me or about the doctors. There is always someone to blame. Sometimes I try to be stoical. I read a journalist talking about getting a terrible disease, and he said that you just have to play with the cards you are given. Sometimes we internalize our anger or fear; we bottle it up; and it feeds depressive illness or mental instability.

David does something we so rarely do. He understands that every mishap, each thing that goes wrong in the world, happens because we are sinners in a world under God's righteous judgment and curse. The particular difficulties don't always come from particular sins, of course. But that's the big picture. As Romans 5:12 will later put it, 'sin came into the world through one man, and death through sin'. We see the shadow of death in problems, from the little difficulties to the huge and grievous sorrows. So the psalmist takes himself to God. He doesn't grumble; he isn't stoical. He doesn't bottle it up; he takes it to the Lord. He knows that God is angry at all human wrongdoing.

I recently read a review of a book by an American pastor. It was pitched as a corrective to the famous sermon preached by Jonathan Edwards in 1741 in New England: *Sinners in the Hands of an Angry God*. If I remember rightly, the new book is called *Sinners in the Hands of a Loving God*. 'We don't want an angry God,' the writer seemed to say. 'No, we want a loving God.' I haven't read the book. But if the review was anything to go by, it was terrible theology. For the Bible teaches that the anger of God is the outworking of his holy love, and his love is inseparable from his anger at sin.

God is – as Article One of the Anglican Thirty-Nine Articles says – 'without body, parts, or passions' (BCP). He is 'without parts'. You cannot construct God in your mind from pre-existing constituent parts of theology. You cannot think of his attributes as building blocks to stick on to his nature. God is who God is; who God is, is what God is. All that is in God is God. His attributes cannot be separated from his being. He does not have love as a quality; he is love. It's not that there is an essential 'godness' of God and that love is one of his attributes. He does not have light; he is light. He does not have holiness; he is holy. Therefore, because his attributes are who God is, you cannot separate them. His love is a holy love. His holiness is a loving holiness. His wrath is a holy loving wrath. His love is a wrathful holy love. His holiness is a loving wrathful holiness. We shouldn't try disassembling God and putting him together again with the parts we like.

In particular, God's anger is inseparable from God's goodness. If God were not angry with evil, God could not be good. If God did not hate evil, he could not be love. If God did not burn with fury against evil, he could not be holy. And David feels this. He feels the pain of being under sin. There's nothing particular he confesses in this psalm. It may not particularly be his sin. I think it quite likely that it isn't, actually. But he knows he is the king of a people under sin. And that hurts.

> Be gracious to me, O LORD, for I am languishing;
>   heal me, O LORD, for my bones are troubled.

My soul also is greatly troubled.
But you, O LORD – how long?

He is languishing and very weak. He is troubled, very troubled, in his bones (his inner strength is ebbing away) and his soul; in his whole person. He cries, 'O LORD, how long?' There is something slow about suffering. It has been said that every experience of the anger of God is a foretaste of the eternity of hell; that's why it feels long. And it's true, isn't it? Our pleasures whistle past us so fast: happy days are soon gone. But in our sorrows, minutes seem like hours, hours like days, days like years: those minutes waiting for the ambulance; that hour in the doctor's waiting room; the days before a dreaded meeting at work; the anticipation of a difficult conversation with a boyfriend or girlfriend – those times just go on and on.

David took the fact that he was a sinner in a world under sin seriously. He knew that every death is because of sin; each disease is the result of sin – often not individual sin, of course, but still sin. Today's mishap, tomorrow's setback, yesterday's sadness: sin lies behind them all, and behind sin is the righteous anger of God. David knew that. We should know that. But there is something more: Jesus knew that. Jesus, the sinless One, carried the burden, the troubled heart, the sorrow of the sin of those for whom he died. He had no sin of his own; but he felt the burden of our sin in all its weight and sadness: 'My soul . . . is greatly troubled.'

It is worth reflecting that the wrath of God hurt Jesus more than God's displeasure can hurt us in this life. It's just a little like this. Imagine a family in which you have a rebellious child and a loyal and obedient child. When the father frowns and says to the difficult child, 'You have done wrong,' that youngster doesn't care very much; he or she is hardened. But when the father says to the loyal one, 'You have disappointed me,' tears will come to his or her eyes. When you and I feel convicted of sin, it should cause us pain. As one nineteenth-century writer put it, 'The tenderer the heart, the deeper the pain [because] a soft heart has goods to lose which a hard one never possessed.'[1]

We have learned to harden ourselves; it takes a work of grace for us to feel the anger of God. But for the soft and tender heart of Jesus, who treasured the Father's love with all his sinless soul, the wrath of God was infinite agony. No wonder his soul was troubled. It was troubled for us. With no sin in his own flawless soul, he felt the weight of the righteous anger of God against sinners. And it troubled his bones and his soul. As Martin Luther said,

> Christ cries out for his people in this way, as if he were the one and he himself were experiencing what happened to them, all because of his exceeding love. Therefore the whole psalm is the lament and voice of our loving Jesus, who went there for us.

Feel the weight of God's wrath, as Jesus did. But we don't end there.

Weep for sins, as Jesus wept (Psalm 6:4–7)

Second, I want us to learn to weep for sins, as Jesus wept. In verses 4–7, David begins to put his troubles into prayer. He begins, 'Turn, O LORD.' There are two kinds of turning in the Bible, the turning of men and women to God in repentance and the turning of God to us in grace. David prays with Spirit-given wisdom for the one that must come first: 'Lord, turn your face to me for, until and unless you turn your face to me, I cannot turn to you in faith.' There's a paradox here; for the prayer is itself the beginning of a turning to God, and yet David knows that the initiative must be with God in his grace: 'Turn, O LORD.'

Have you ever *tried* to repent? It's really hard. 'I'm going to turn over a new leaf. I'm going to fight that sin – that grumbling, that bitterness, that lust, that resentment. I'm going to turn from it.' But then, as Augustine wrote, 'We find it a tough and uphill struggle to twist ourselves away from the gloom of earthbound desires.'[2] We need God to turn to us if we are ever to turn to him.

Although this is traditionally a penitential psalm, there is no explicit confession of David's sin (unlike, for example, in Psalm 51 or Psalm 38). The grief David feels is for a world under sin, a world under the righteous anger of God. For David, that includes his own sins, as it does for us. For Jesus, it is the sins of all for whom he suffers. Jesus never repents of his own sin, for he had none. But he turns his face to the Father, day after day, and pleads with his Father to turn his face to him.

In verse 5, he gives a reason: in death, in Sheol, the place of the dead, people can't praise God. David lives to praise God. Jesus lives to make the Father known, to praise him. If David dies and stays dead for ever, God will be praised less; God's glory will be compromised. If that is unthinkable, how much more so if Jesus dies and stays dead? Who will give God praise? Who will make the Father known? God is the God of the living, so there must be resurrection (as Jesus taught).

In verses 6 and 7, David weeps and weeps. He uses extraordinarily strong language. The eye is a kind of index of life. We talk about a twinkle in the eye. But now his eye wastes away. These are the dull eyes of the sufferer; the terrible, empty eyes people have when someone they love has died. David feels the grief of sins. Calvin wrote that it is as if David 'sees hell open to receive him, and the mental distress which this produces exceeds all other sorrows.'[3] But, again, there is more. Jesus wept. He wept at the grave of Lazarus. He wept over Jerusalem. He was overwhelmed with sorrow in Gethsemane. He prayed 'with loud cries and tears' (Hebrews 5:7). He wept and he wept and he wept. I do not think we can even begin to know how much Jesus wept for sins.

Let me ask you, as I ask myself: have you ever wept for sins? The other day, Carolyn and I were meeting with friends to pray about a very painful thing – a Christian had fallen into sin. As we talked, I noticed tears in the eyes of our friend, not just tears of sadness but tears for the misery of sin. That is what it means to walk in the footsteps of

Jesus. Have you ever been haunted by the memory of some sin in your own life, perhaps long ago? Maybe there were wasted years before you came to Christ, and you look back on them with sadness. Perhaps there was something you said that you deeply regret, or some lust, unfaithfulness, greed, malice or deceit – and the memory weighs heavily on you. You think, 'I so wish I had not said that, seen that, done that. How can God love me?' One old writer says, 'Satan can better endure his own fire than our tears, and he is more racked by the weeping of a contrite heart than by the flame of the burning of hell.'[4] For when he sees men or women weeping for their sin, he knows he is losing them.

It will be well if you and I learn to weep for sins – supremely for our own sins but also for the sins of others. When we do, let us remember the Scottish writer Andrew Bonar's words: 'If you have felt anguish of spirit under a sense of deserved wrath, let it cease when you find the Man of Sorrows presenting all his anguish as the atonement for your soul.'[5] As we sing in the old hymn:

He took my sins and my sorrows,
and made them his very own.
He bore the burden to Calvary
and suffered and died alone.[6]

It is good to weep for tears now for, as John Chrysostom put it, 'If you do not weep here, you will weep after death, but to no good purpose. But if you weep here, you will be consoled,' which is just what Psalm 6:8–10 shows. If you set verses 1–7 to music, it must be in a minor key. It is very sad. But now there is a sudden change. Now there is confidence, assurance and authority. Now the trumpets sound!

Be sure of freedom from sin, as you hear Jesus speak (Psalm 6:8–10)

The King speaks: 'Depart from me, all you workers of evil' (verse 8). Does that remind you of anything? 'On that day,' says Jesus at the end of the Sermon on the Mount, '[people who thought they were insiders] will say to me, "Lord, Lord . . ." And then I will declare to them, "I never knew you; depart from me, you workers of lawlessness"' (Matthew 7:22–23). That's our second echo (see p. 41 for the first one). Again, in Luke 13:27, to the same people, the Son of Man will say, 'Depart from me, all you workers of evil!' David the King says this. In the end, Jesus the King says this: 'Depart from me! Go! Scram! Away! For ever!'

It is a paradox that, at the end of the psalm, the Jesus who felt the anger of God against sinners now expresses the anger of God against impenitent sinners. In his human nature, he felt that wrath; in his divine nature, he now demonstrates it in final judgment. How can he say this? Because he knows God hears his prayers. Three times, he says this:

> for the LORD has heard the sound of my weeping.
> The LORD has heard my plea;
>   the LORD accepts my prayer.

'Ask of me' (Psalm 2:8); pray and I will answer. The King who prays is the King who weeps for sins, who hates sin, who feels the sadness of sin. And God in heaven hears his prayer.

One day, at the end of time, the Son of Man will speak these words of confident authority to all who will not turn from sin: 'Depart from me!' So, he can be sure that, 'All my enemies shall be ashamed and greatly troubled' (Psalm 6:10). You can either have a troubled soul for sins in this life or a greatly troubled soul for eternity.

'They shall turn back and be put to shame in a moment' – in a moment. For when judgment comes, it will be too late to repent; see Psalm 2:12, where it says that 'his wrath is quickly kindled'. God is patient but he will not wait for ever. The suffering of God's King seems so slow: 'How long?' Yet the judgment of God's enemies will happen 'in a moment'.

It is worth pondering those words: 'Depart from me.' They call, I think, for us to acknowledge three things.

A warning

The first is a warning. Jesus says he will speak these words to people who thought they were insiders. 'Lord, Lord,' they say, 'did we not prophesy in your name?' (Matthew 7:22). He speaks those terrible words to those who are in church but not in Christ. He speaks them to false teachers. He speaks them to hypocrites. He speaks them to all who will not repent and weep for sins. So let us first search our hearts to make our calling and election sure.

A challenge

The second is a challenge. In this life, we should long to distance ourselves from sin. We have to fight the good fight of faith in our own hearts, not give up on the battle against our own sins. But, sometimes, we may need to distance ourselves from the fellowship of sinners. We will and must be in the world, but we must not share the world's values. In particular (Jesus teaches this in Matthew 18, and Paul follows Jesus' teaching in 1 Corinthians 5), when sin gets into the church, we must exercise church discipline. 'Depart from us' may sometimes mean 'you have to be put out of fellowship that you may learn afresh to repent of some sin'. That 'depart from us' may be an echo of the words of Jesus the Head of the Church: 'Depart from me.'

A warning. A challenge.

Comfort

But I think our main acknowledgement needs to be that these words offer us wonderful comfort. We long to be freed from sin. We feel the sadness that sin brings into the world. We lament the darkness in our own hearts. How wonderful that Jesus our King will one day speak those words of authority – 'Depart from me!' – and that the human race will be divided into those who grieve at sins and those who care little about sins. Jesus, who weeps for sins, will gather into his kingdom every man, every woman and every child who has been grieved by sin; not just for the consequences of sin (for we all grieve for those) but for sin in all its ugliness. My friend, if sin grieves you, there is hope because Jesus wept for sins and for sinners.

Let me close with a very old prayer:

> We know, O Lord Jesus Christ, that while you were on earth, you did every night water your couch with tears for us: grant us so to repent for our iniquities, that we may hereafter attain to that place where all tears are wiped from all eyes.[7]

Notes

1. John Brown, *Expository Discourses on the First Epistle of the Apostle Peter* (William Olliphant and Sons, 1849), p. 484.
2. Quoted in Craig A. Blaising and Carmen S. Hardin (eds.), *Psalms 1 – 50*, Ancient Christian Commentary on Scripture, Old Testament VII (IVP, 2008), p. 50.
3. Herman J. Selderhuis, *Psalms 1 – 72*, Reformation Commentary on Scripture (IVP, 2015), p. 58.
4. Rev. J. M. Neale, *Rev. J. M. Neale Collection* (Aeterna Press, 2016).
5. Andrew Bonar, *Christ and His Church in the Book of Psalms* (Scholarly Publishing Office, 2005), p. 22.
6. Charles Hutchinson Gabriel (1856–1932), 'I stand amazed in the presence'.
7. Neale, *Rev. J. M. Neale Collection*.

The Seminars

Our Future Hope

Michael Reeves

Michael Reeves is President and Professor of Theology at Union School of Theology. He is the author of numerous books including *The Good God*, *Christ Our Life*, *Enjoy Your Prayer Life* and *The Unquenchable Flame*. He is the Director of the European Theologians Network, and speaks and teaches regularly worldwide. Formerly, he was Head of Theology for the Universities and Colleges Christian Fellowship (UCCF) and an associate minister at All Souls Church, Langham Place, London. He is married to Bethan and they have two daughters.

I'd like you to imagine you're an Israelite in the days of Moses, leaving Egypt, and it is Yom Kippur – the great Day of Atonement. Aaron, the high priest, dressed in pure linen, has just sacrificed the goat for the sin offering. Now, that should be a familiar moment to you. We recognize that Day of Atonement sacrifice as a picture, a type, of Jesus' sacrifice on the cross. What would happen next, on the Day of Atonement, was that the high priest would take the blood of that sacrifice behind the veil into the holy of holies, in the tabernacle, and he would sprinkle it over the mercy seat. That again is a picture we recognize of the true High Priest, Christ, taking the blood of his offering into the true holy of holies, the true tabernacle in heaven itself, there to offer himself and his sacrifice before God his Father.

We are standing now in this very special Day of Atonement, held only once every fiftieth year. Every fifty years, when the high priest would take the blood and disappear into the holy of holies, all the people would hold their breath. You would have been able to hear a pin drop because a once-in-a-lifetime event was about to happen. The high priest would disappear behind the veil and then, when his work was done, he would step back out. When he stepped back out, a trumpet would sound. Leviticus 25 tells us about it: 'on the Day of Atonement sound the trumpet throughout your land. Consecrate the fiftieth year and proclaim liberty throughout the land to all its inhabitants. It shall be a jubilee for you' (Leviticus 25:9–10). So, the high priest would go in to the holy of holies to make atonement and, when he stepped back out, a trumpet would sound, announcing jubilee. In that year of jubilee, debts would be cancelled, slaves would be freed and the very land itself would be allowed to rest, so no sowing or reaping would be done. It was to be a foretaste of the Bible's cosmic hope, the time when all our debt would be cancelled, all our bondage to sin would be ended; when the meek would inherit the earth.

Does any of this sound familiar – the awaited high priest reappearing; the trumpet sounding, announcing an atonement-bought rest? The Lord himself will descend from heaven with the sound of the trumpet: 'the trumpet will sound, the dead [in Christ] will be raised imperishable' (1 Corinthians 15:52). It should sound familiar because just as the high priest's going into the holy of holies was the picture of Christ's ascension to heaven, so the high priest's return was a picture of Christ's, especially in the jubilee year. In those little details, we find a truckload of comfort because we see that it is the very same man who went into the holy of holies who steps back out. The man who goes into heaven is the same man who comes back out. As the angels told those gaping disciples when Jesus ascended: 'This same Jesus, who has been taken from you into heaven, will come back in the same way you have seen him go into heaven' (Acts 1:11).

It was the same high priest who returned from the holy of holies; it's the same man who will return from heaven. When the trumpet sounds and the judge of all the earth appears, we will see the same one who died to make atonement for us – there's the great, comforting application for Christians. He's the one we wait for.

A glorious day of judgment

Question 52 of the Heidelberg Catechism puts the issue very directly and asks, 'What comfort is it to you that Christ shall return to judge the living and the dead?' It's strikingly phrased, isn't it, because you could expect 'How scary is it to you that Christ shall come to return to judge the living and the dead?' But it doesn't ask that; it says, 'What comfort is it to you?' The answer you're supposed to give is this:

> [What comfort is it to me? That] in all my sorrow[s] and persecution, I lift my head and [wait] eagerly . . . from heaven the very same person who . . . submitted himself to the judgment of God . . . and has removed all the curse from me.[1]

That's who we wait for – the judge of all the earth is the one who died in screaming agony on the cross for us. So, when he returns, brothers and sisters, do you think he could forget us? Do you think he could reject us, given the blood he spilled for us? No. So Christians confidently long for the day of the judge to come. We are a people known for crying, 'Your kingdom come! *Maranatha!* Come, Lord Jesus!' We are a people who eagerly await the 'blessed hope – the appearing of the glory of our great God and Saviour, Jesus Christ' (Titus 2:13).

It is as it was, before Joshua took the people into the Promised Land. Do you remember? The Canaanites were so depraved that they would burn their sons and daughters as sacrifices to their gods. They made the very land retch at their presence, so foully depraved were they. The sounding of the trumpets at Jericho meant a judgment that would be deliverance – the evil would be removed for the healing of the land that the people of God would inherit. Just so, Jesus is our true Joshua ('Jesus' is the Greek form of the Hebrew name 'Joshua'). He is our Joshua who comes to cleanse the earth for his people. It's why 'creation waits in eager expectation' (Romans 8:19) for that day because his judgment means the destruction of evil for the renewal of this creation.

On that great day, all those believers who have gone to be with him already, will return with him, now in his victory train; we who are left will be caught up with them and we will sing a victory song. With the martyrs, with departed parents, spouses and with all the cloud of witnesses, we will cry:

Where, O death, is your victory?
    Where, O death, is your sting?
(1 Corinthians 15:55)

Death has been swallowed up in victory.
(1 Corinthians 15:54)

So, the day of Christ's return will be a glorious day of judgment. It will be a judgment we can look forward to, confident in Christ, eagerly awaiting the full victory of his righteousness over everything that is evil in us, which will be removed, and over everything that is wrong in creation.

A day of gorgeous transformation

It will also be a day of gorgeous transformation, when his eternal purpose to perfect a people for himself will be complete. You see, already, by the Spirit, he is transforming us. Think of 2 Corinthians 3:18: 'we all, with unveiled face, beholding the glory of the Lord, are being transformed into [his] image from one degree of glory to another' (ESV). So, contemplating him by faith, we are, right now, being transformed into his likeness, but on *that* day, when Christ actually reappears – when we clap eyes on him physically at his second coming – then, 1 John 3:2 says, 'we shall be like him, for we shall see him as he is'. So, the sight of him now, by faith, begins to transform us spiritually, but the sight of him then, face to face, will finally make us like him, body and soul. That full, unveiled physical sight of the glorified Jesus will be so majestically affecting that our bodies will transform around us. When we see him in the full sweetness and awesomeness of his glory, when we behold *him*, it will mean the blasting away of all the sin and pain that is in us. Theologians used to call that sight the 'beatific vision' because it will be the most 'happifying' sight.

We need to dwell on this because we need to be careful when we talk about all the many, many blessings that the Lord will bring on his return. Our constant danger is that we will set our hearts on the blessings and not on him; that we'll long for the messianic banquet but not the Messiah; we'll want the crowns but not the King. But before all else, the delight of the saints in glory is the enjoyment, the head-filling, heart-melting adoration of *him*.

Actually, when saints are in their right mind now, that's how it is. You may remember, Paul wrote to the Philippians and he told them, 'My desire is to depart and be' – he doesn't say 'in heaven'; he says, 'My desire is to depart and be with Christ, [which] is far better' (Philippians 1:23 ESV), because, for Paul, heaven would not be heaven without Christ. The bride longs to be with her bridegroom; that's what the church longs for, as the bride of Christ, we long to be with the Bridegroom. More than anything else our hope is to be with him. *God* will be the glory and delight of the saints; that's what we've been designed for; that's the heart of the eternal life for which we've been saved. God the Father has eternally enjoyed gazing upon the perfection of his Son. On the day Jesus returns, the Father will allow us fully to share his own happiness in Christ.

That is why our bodies will transform – because we'll see him. That's why we'll have perfect life and joy – because we will be with him. Christ is the jewel in the crown of our hope. He is the fountainhead, the source of all the blessings of the new creation. The creation will become a thoroughly good place because every knee will bow to him. Where, right now, sin makes things eccentric, off-balance, wrong – around Jesus, all things will find what they were meant to be.

Just as unbelievers don't understand why Christians would look forward to that day, they equally don't believe it's going to happen because there is no obvious indication of it in the world. As the years roll on, the world doesn't look any less spoilt or more peaceful. Here's the thing we need to remember, friends: amid all the world-shaking that's going on around us, our confidence does not come from looking at the world; it comes from Jesus. The ever-faithful God of truth has promised and 'no matter how many promises God has made, they are "Yes" in Christ' (2 Corinthians 1:20). There is more, in fact, than just a promise; the clock is ticking. The new creation has already begun. Raised from death to a new life, Christ is now the firstborn, the firstfruit of new life, the head of the new creation. So, his resurrection two thousand years ago has started an irreversible tide of life, and it is a tide that will sweep through all creation. Isaac Watts put it like this in his great classic hymn 'Joy to the world':

> Joy to the world; the Lord is come;
> Let earth receive her King:
> Let every heart prepare Him room,
> And heaven and nature sing . . .
>
> No more let sins and sorrows grow,
> Nor thorns infest the ground . . .

Here are, perhaps, my favourite lines:

> He comes to make His blessings flow
> Far as the curse is found . . .[2]

When Christ returns, he will finally and completely undo the fall here, in this world that he made.

In Genesis 3, sin brought death; it brought pain in childbirth; it brought marital difficulties; it meant an earth that was hard to work, full of thorns and thistles; and he comes to make his blessings flow as far as all that curse is found. And he returns here, to his creation that he once declared good, now spoiled by sin, to overturn and heal all that brokenness. So, the heavens and the earth – the whole cosmos – will be restored and revived. It means, brothers and sisters, that our hope is not pie in the sky when we die. We will go to Christ when we die (if we die before he returns) but our hope is to return with him, to be in that victory train, to see *these* trees, *these* fields, *this* creation renewed because the One through whom all things were made will undo the chaos; he will mend and bind his original handiwork back together. In Matthew 19:28, Jesus called it 'the renewal of all things, when the Son of Man [will sit] on his glorious throne'. It's why Paul tells us, in Romans 8:22–23, 'that the whole creation has been groaning as in the [pangs] of childbirth . . . as we wait eagerly for our adoption as sons, the redemption of our bodies' (NIV84), because our hope is to see *this* creation, not that it is thrown away and we go elsewhere. Christ's people will return with him here, to creation renewed; that is our hope.

In fact, this doesn't mean that he will merely restore Eden. The story of the gospel is not just paradise regained. When the Son of Man sits on his glorious throne, it will be better than Eden when Adam was in charge because Jesus is better than Adam. So, there will be more glory in the days of the Son of Man than ever there were in the days of the first man, because as the last Adam is so much superior to the first, so will his reign be. The first man, Adam, was made to rule over creation; everything was put under his feet, and he fell and all creation fell with him. What about the last man, the last Adam, the Son of Man? Well, behold, says Daniel 7:13–14:

> before me was one like a son of man, coming with the clouds of heaven. He approached the Ancient of Days and was led into his presence. He was given authority, glory and sovereign power; all nations and peoples of every language worshipped him. His dominion is an everlasting dominion that will not pass away, and his kingdom is one that will never be destroyed.

What a difference! Oh, it had been good, before Adam fell, completely good, but he was fallible. He had only what Paul called 'a natural body' (1 Corinthians 15:44). In Adam's day, there was a tree to avoid, a threat of a serpent; with Christ, we have so much more. We are not mere creatures but the adopted children of God, sharing the beloved Son's own life and righteous status. He is infallibly faithful. He has a glorious, imperishable body that has defeated death. Paul called it 'a spiritual body' in 1 Corinthians 15:44, the sort of body we will have when these bodies of ours are transformed and perfected. When he appears in that body, there will be no threats left. There will be only the tree of life; there will be no serpent to threaten us. Dear brothers and sisters, with Christ, we have a hope that outstrips Eden itself.

Right now, yes, we see so evidently the creation sliding back into the wilful darkness. Then, Christ will drive that darkness away and creation will be suffused with the bright glory of Christ. It will share the liberation of the children of God. In that day, when we've returned with Christ *here*, to enjoy *his* reign *here*, the sound of weeping will no longer be heard. The lion will lie down with the lamb; the desert will bloom like the rose; the ploughman will overtake the reaper; mountains will run with new wine (see Isaiah 11:6; 35:1–2; Amos 9:13); and a man – this time the faithful man, at peace with the Ancient of Days – will reign in this paradise. This Son of Man's wonderful rule will never fail. It will never be destroyed.

Notes

1. <www.heidelberg-catechism.com/en/lords-days/19.html>.
2. Isaac Watts, 1674–1748.

Hope and Grief

Joanna Jackson

Dr Joanna Jackson is currently serving as Director of Counselling at All Souls Church, Langham Place, London. She is a counselling psychologist by training and has also trained in biblical counselling. She is married to a church pastor, has four children and lives in London.

What comes into your mind when you think of the word 'grief'? I expect that most of us associate it with the death of a loved one, which, most certainly, is an experience that provokes grief of the deepest kind. But grief can follow the loss of almost anything: the loss of a relationship, a job, a home or an expectation. Grief is the response to that loss. It is described in the Bible as sorrow, mourning or lament. And, while it is primarily an emotional response, it is not just limited to our emotions but affects our mind, behaviour and physical well-being (appetite, sleep and energy levels); it is a whole-person response to loss.

I'm aware that there will be people engaging with the Virtually Keswick Convention who are grieving in a particularly acute and deep way at the moment. For others of us, grief may not be so intense but, in light of the pandemic, I expect that we will all have experienced grief in some shape or form: over the past months, many of us have faced the loss of financial security, the loss of connection with others, and the loss of normal routines and patterns of life. The way we study, work, shop and socialize – all of these things have been rewritten, along with our summer holiday plans!

I know people who have had to cancel weddings and close businesses. I know women who have had to give birth by themselves because husbands were not allowed on to hospital wards. I know of operations that have been cancelled or treatments postponed. I know about marriages that have come under enormous strain during lockdown. I know people who have lost husbands, fathers, mothers, sisters and friends; people whose funerals had to take place online or in such a way that their loved ones weren't even able to receive a hug or a handshake at a time they needed it most. There have been all sorts of losses during a time like this.

Now, the Bible isn't arranged by topic. We can't go to a section labelled 'grief', let alone 'grief during a pandemic'. But the whole Bible story is one of loss followed by restoration, of grief and hope. As well as the overarching picture, there are many passages of Scripture that speak specifically about grief. I thought it would be useful to base ourselves in one particular passage for our time today: 1 Peter 1:3–9.

Grief is to be expected

The first thing I want to draw our attention to from this passage is that grief is to be expected. Peter writes, 'though now for a little while you may have had to suffer grief in all kinds of trials' (verse 6). He was writing to Christians who were living in a society that was becoming increasingly hostile to their faith. Does that sound familiar? They were being slandered and maligned. Their family relationships and livelihoods were being threatened. They were facing trials and grieving because of this.

We know from Scripture and experience that persecution isn't the only trial we face. There are 'all kinds of trials' that come from simply living in a fallen world. The arrival of sin into this world – the wilful rebellion of God's children against their Creator, starting with Adam and Eve – brought death, judgment and brokenness into every aspect, every sphere and every element of life. Physical death is now a reality for everyone. The shadow of death, which is seen and experienced in 'all kinds of trials' – from disappointments to disease, from depression to divorce – leaves no one untouched. Covid-19 is one small example of God's judgment and a painful reminder of the awfulness and intrusiveness of sin. In a world full of 'all kinds of trials', Peter reminds us that grief is normal; it is to be expected.

Within the psychological world, there has been discussion about how we have been grieving, both individually and collectively, over the things we have lost as a result of Covid-19. And I wonder whether one of the reasons why the pandemic has been so disorientating, especially for us in the West, is because we don't expect grief. There is a narrative in our society that life should get better and better. There is an expectation that we will go from strength to strength: get a better job, earn more money, become more successful. There can be a positive spin given to almost anything.

Under normal circumstances, death is rarely talked about. We try our best to ignore the fact that we will all die sooner or later. And yet the pandemic has brought death to our doorstep. I'm sure I am not the only one who, early on in lockdown, spent time looking at statistics and working out how likely I was to die, according to my age bracket, if I contracted the virus.

In our society, we don't expect trials and grief feels far from normal. As a church, we may be more comfortable talking about death but, when it comes to dealing with grief, we often fall short. I met with someone who was grieving the loss of her child and she told me how people didn't know what to say to her or how to treat her in church. Either they would just be awkward or would try to comfort her by helping her look on the bright side, giving her theological platitudes:

'God will work out all things for your good.'

'Keep focusing on all the other blessings you still have.'

'I am sure God will give you another child.'

Even though they meant well, it was very difficult for people to actually engage with her grief, to mourn with her.

Everyone is sinful and suffering in some way. One of the privileges of doing my job is that I hear about some of these burdens. Some people may walk into church and think that everyone has it together, that to be a Christian means that they should always be smiling and looking on the bright side of life. Others avoid church because they are in a season when tears come too easily and they would feel awkward crying in church. And yet the Bible tells us that trials are normal, that grief is to be expected.

Now that may sound pretty depressing but I think there is some encouragement to be taken from this. Recognizing that grief is to be expected frees us from thinking that there is something uniquely wrong with us or our lives when we face trouble and loss.

The world tells us that if only we buy the right things, meet the right person, raise the right children, pursue the right career and take the right vitamins, we will be free from hardship and grief. But it's not true. This world is not our home.

Peter talks about an inheritance in heaven 'that can never perish, spoil or fade' (verse 4). This is an encouragement precisely because the things on earth do perish, spoil and fade. So, when trials and grief come your way, don't think that God is singling you out for some special kind of torture or that you are necessarily doing something wrong to cause your trials. Trials are inevitable. Grief is to be expected.

Not only that but knowing that grief is to be expected means that we don't have to pretend that everything is always fine. To be a Christian doesn't mean that you should be continually smiling or that the command to 'rejoice always' (1 Thessalonians 5:16) leaves no room for sadness and mourning. There is nothing unspiritual about grief. You are not failing as a Christian because you are experiencing sorrow and sadness. Quite the opposite. The gospel gives us permission to grieve because it is the right response to a world under judgment.

Lastly, recognizing that grief is to be expected frees us from a wrong understanding of the gospel. To follow Jesus doesn't mean we will be protected from hardship and loss. When we face trouble, it is not that God is somehow letting us down, has stopped loving us, stopped being good or has broken his promises. I know a number of people whose faith has been shipwrecked on the rocks of trials because they thought that God was not keeping up his end of the bargain; that, somehow, he owed them a life free from trials and grief. So when they faced the unexpected loss of someone or something they held dear, they turned away from him.

It may be worth taking some time to ask yourself which gospel you are believing because God hasn't promised us a loss-free, grief-free existence here and now. But for the Christian, for his children, he has promised us that grief is not the end.

Grief is not the end

Peter writes:

> In his great mercy he has given us a new birth into a living hope through the resurrection of Jesus Christ from the dead, and into an inheritance that can never perish, spoil or fade. This inheritance is kept in heaven for you.
> (1 Peter 1:3–4)

The moment we put our trust in Christ, we were given new birth into a living hope. Not a dead hope that is nothing more than wishful thinking but a hope that is alive through the resurrection of Jesus Christ from the dead. Jesus' resurrection is the foundation of our faith. Because he rose from the dead, our hope is guaranteed. Just as Jesus now lives for evermore, so our hope is ever-living.

It has been said that 'cynicism is, increasingly, the dominant spirit of our age'.[1] Cynicism – an attitude in which you don't invest emotionally in anything – is a protection mechanism because, if you don't care, you are less likely to get hurt. If you don't hope, you won't be disappointed. I have to admit, I have sympathy for this point of view. But, as Christians, we should never be cynical when it comes to our hope in Christ because it will in no way disappoint. His resurrection points us to a day when death, mourning, sorrow and pain will be no more; when sin, struggle and suffering will be done away with; when everything that was lost will be restored; when everything that is broken will be mended; and when everything that is sad will be undone. We, and this world, will be made new and more glorious, and even the best things in this world will seem like shadows. And, more wonderful than anything else, we will see our Father face to face. We will no longer have to struggle to walk by faith because we will see him with our own eyes.

This hope we have in Christ doesn't get rid of grief in trials, but it guarantees that – no matter how deep or wearisome our grief is here and now, no matter how endless it seems – it will not last for ever. The Lord has put a time limit on it. Those in Christ know that a day is coming when every tear will be wiped away (Revelation 21:4) and those who mourn will be comforted (Matthew 5:4).

'Weeping may stay for the night, but rejoicing comes in the morning' (Psalm 30:5). This means that the grief in trials we experience now really is only for 'a little while' (1 Peter 1:6). I love the way Peter describes grief because he makes it sound so trivial and limited. It certainly doesn't feel like it in the moment, but that really is what it is. It's only for a little while. The resurrection of Christ stands as a guarantee that death and all the shadows of death will die, that what awaits us will never perish, spoil or fade, and our future – our living hope – will one day be revealed.

We need to cling to these great and precious promises because, when you are in the midst of grief, it seems as if it will never end. I know people in deep depression who can't see the light at the end of the tunnel. I know people who have been so hurt by life that they are afraid to cry because, if they start, they fear they might never stop. But no matter how strong our feelings or how bleak the situation, we have hope. So, cling on to it. Memorize these promises. Bind them to your heart. Speak about them. Sing about them. Talk to the Lord about them: 'This feels overwhelming. It feels like I can't cope. But help me Lord, today, to keep believing; to trust that this will end and a better day is coming. Help me to cling on to the hope you give me in Jesus.'

Grief is to be expected but, for the Christian, it is not the end. So, what does it look like to grieve in the light of our hope?

Grieving in hope

There are lots of things we could say here but let me just highlight a couple of applications from our first two points. The first way to grieve in hope is to lament. The distinctive way that we grieve as Christians – as opposed to the rest of the world – is that we bring our grief to the Lord. He doesn't call us to bear it silently or stoically ignore it. We aren't only to unload it to a therapist or friend. We are to bring it to the Lord. The Bible's word for this is 'lament'. Part of the reason why the psalms are so precious to people who are in pain is because they are filled with lament, with people crying out to God, complaining about their trials, questioning God, pleading for him to act. The psalms of lament show us what it looks like to grieve well as a Christian. They are raw and honest, sometimes uncomfortably so, but they are prayers and songs of faith precisely because they are spoken to the Lord.

One of my favourite verses is Psalm 62:8, which says, 'Trust in him at all times, you people; pour out your hearts to him, for God is our refuge.' Learning how to pour out your heart to the Lord in lament is one of the key ways that we, as Christians, grieve in hope. And, if you want to walk alongside someone who is grieving – to mourn with those who mourn – then learning to lament is where you should start. After all, the psalms were designed to be said or sung collectively. We can lament on our own and together.

The second way to grieve in hope is to look to Jesus. When life is hard, while we may know theologically that comfort is found in Jesus, we often turn to other things. We try to distract ourselves by binge watching Netflix, immersing ourselves in work, seeking comfort in a bottle of wine or chocolate. We might even try to alleviate our pain and disappointment through pornography, self-harm or material things. While these might provide some welcome relief, it is only momentary and often leaves us feeling emptier. There is only one person who can provide the comfort that restores your heart – the source of all true comfort – Jesus Christ, because he knows your pain.

In Jesus, we have a friend who did not remain distant in heaven. He did not protect himself from loss but entered this world and experienced pain and grief in the profoundest of ways. He lost material comfort and financial security. He wept at the graveside of friends. He was let down by those he was closest to in the world. Ultimately, he bore the weight of sin and, on the cross, experienced the incomprehensible loss of his Father's love: 'My God, my God, why have you forsaken me?' (Matthew 27:46).

Jesus experienced more grief than anyone else. Isaiah describes him as 'a man of sorrows, and acquainted with grief' (Isaiah 53:3 ESV). And he did it for us. He was forsaken so that we might be forgiven. He gave up everything so that we might gain everything. He subjected himself to grief so that we might have hope, to ensure that, no matter what trials we face, we will never grieve alone. So, keep looking to Jesus, pour out your heart to him, knowing that he is with you. This is how we grieve in hope.

This seminar was followed by a Q&A session with Joanna Jackson.

How should we relate to people who are grieving? What should we say?

Great question. I suppose what I often bear in mind is how Jesus related to people who were grieving. In particular, I think of his responses to Mary and Martha at the death of their brother Lazarus. You'll remember that, with Mary, he wept; with Martha, he spoke truth and pointed her to the resurrection of the dead. We all need both of those; we all need people who will weep with us and people who will speak truth to our hearts, to reassure us, to comfort us. We'll probably have different tendencies: some of us are more likely to speak more truth; some of us are more likely to do the weeping. But, I suppose, it's best to bear both of those in mind.

A few follow-up comments about that: learning how to listen well to someone is really important; communicating that you want to hear, that you want to understand and that you are with them. Mourning alongside them is something that is so valuable and such a precious gift to someone who is facing loss and sorrow. It's important to be able to do that well but also not to be afraid, at the right time, with gentleness and compassion, to point them to Jesus. Perhaps ask if you can pray with them or for them. Carefully considering a verse or a passage that communicates God's love and his presence with them is also something that, I think, would be a wonderful thing to do.

How do we help someone who's not a Christian to grieve?

In many ways, all of those things, I think, apply. There's obviously a fundamental difference that someone who isn't a Christian doesn't have that sure hope. But I would still say you want to communicate God's love for them by being with them in their grief. You know what? That's something that people who don't have hope find very difficult to do. It's difficult to mourn with people. I think knowing that God is your strength means that you actually can get into the pit alongside them.

Also, I would say, don't be afraid to speak of Jesus. But we also need to be aware that when a non-Christian is grieving, it's not the time to think, 'Great! They're at their most vulnerable; now's the time to win them for Christ!' Now is not necessarily the time. We don't want to take advantage of someone who is very vulnerable. I would often pray about it. Ask for permission. Ask if they would be willing for you to pray for them. Tentatively ask if you could share something that is a comfort to you. Pray that you might show them something of God's immense love for them in the midst of their grief and their loss.

What do you think is the best way to support someone who is grieving for someone who did not believe in Christ?

This is an incredibly painful situation to be in. If that's asked by a particular person who is facing such a situation, then my heart goes out to them. I'm sure all of us are likely, at one point or another, to face this situation.

I don't think there's any easy answer, but the Lord is good and the Lord is just. We are called, even when we don't understand it, to put our hope and our trust in him, and know that he will do right. With any grief (as well as when grieving for a non-Christian), the Lord calls you to come to him, to pour out your heart to him. Don't be afraid to tell him all your doubts, your fears, your concerns, your anger, your regrets – all of that he longs to hear and he will be with you in it. Remember his heart: he wept over Jerusalem; he longs for the lost to come to him. It breaks his heart when someone dies not trusting in the Lord Jesus. But, ultimately, that's not our decision to make and we don't know what might have happened in those last hours or minutes for that person. We are simply called to put our trust in the Lord and to depend on him.

You mentioned as an aside that the pandemic was a judgment of sin. Can you briefly unpack the relationship between judgment, sin and suffering?

The world is broken. It's fundamentally broken because of our sin and because of God's judgment. The pandemic is most certainly evidence of God's judgment. But I say that with one big caution – that it is not a personal judgment. As Jesus reminded us in the Gospels, it's not a personal judgment on any individual but it is a demonstration – a wake-up call – to the world that we have a broken relationship with the Lord; yet he is calling us back to him. So, yes, it is God's judgment and we can't shy away from that. He's been patient in giving us these warning signs, beckoning us to come to him. But by no means is it a personal judgment on any particular individual that they are somehow more sinful than someone else and, therefore, have been hurt more deeply by the pandemic than others.

My sister died a year ago today from cancer. It was wonderful to see her faith grow through the suffering she faced, and ours too. Is it odd that we feel more bereft now, a year on, than we did at first?

I'm sorry to hear about your loss. I would say no, it's actually really common to feel more bereft later on. When someone dies, there's initially so much to do; there's so much change taking place. There are lots of things to focus our attention on connected with the person that we lost: planning a funeral; sorting out their belongings. Not only that, everyone else knows that you've just experienced this loss and comes to your aid. They will be asking you about it, praying for you, perhaps bringing you meals. You'll be very much in people's minds. It's very present.

As time goes by, things move on for other people. Yet they don't for your sister; they don't for the person we've lost. In one sense, they don't for you as the person who is bereaved. You are still facing that loss every day. It's harder when other things move on and, yet, you haven't been able to move on.

So, no, I don't think it's uncommon. Perhaps it's a reminder for us all, who are looking after others who have lost loved ones, to keep that in mind. A year on, two years on, actually to still be asking them about their loss, asking how we can pray for them, pointing them to the hope we have in Jesus. For us, as we experience that loss, we have to be patient with ourselves, be kind, because that is how God treats us. Keep going and keep looking to him.

Is there a time period after which it's helpful to seek professional help or a point at which you think, actually, you should do that now?
Interestingly, at least within the NHS, it's often advised not to have counselling or therapy after bereavement for at least six months. That guideline is put in place because there is a sort of 'normal' process to grieving, to loss, that takes time. While often those initial stages are very difficult and painful, and we think we need all the support we can get, actually that's not necessarily the time to seek professional help. Yet, there may well be a time, if the grief is complicated by other things, to do so.

I would say, though, don't neglect to make the best use of your family and friends. So, while I absolutely wholeheartedly believe that professional help is a gift of God to the church, and there may well be a good time to seek that out (and I would do so first and foremost by talking to your GP about it), also turn to your church family. Ask people for the help that you need. Don't be afraid to communicate how you feel to others, asking them for prayer. Seek wise counsel from people who love you, know you, will walk with you and support you no matter what.

So, by all means seek professional help but do so with your church family supporting you all the way.

Is the Christian hope just jam for tomorrow?

By 'jam for tomorrow', I presume you mean we just hold on to heaven and the rest of life is difficult. I would say no. There, of course, is this wonderful hope, that God will make all things right, that we look forward to. But here and now, fundamentally, we have the Holy Spirit, who is the greatest gift to us. He assures us of God's love for us, his presence with us and that he will never leave us nor forsake us – no matter what we go through. He gives us purpose, here and now, knowing that God will use everything. Nothing will be wasted, not even our sorrow. We have a calling to continue to live for Jesus and the Holy Spirit gives us power to do so, no matter what we are facing.

Note

1. Paul Millar, *A Praying Life: Connecting with God in a Distracting World* (NavPress, 2009), p. 77.

Hope and Lament

Rico Villanueva

Rico Villanueva gained his PhD in Old Testament from Trinity College, Bristol. He serves as Regional Commissioning Editor for Langham Publications and as Scholar Care Coordinator for current Langham scholars in Asia. He is the author of several books, including *It's OK to Be Not OK: Preaching the Lament Psalms* and commentaries on the books of Psalms and Lamentations – all published by Langham.

'God is good! All the time!' I often hear this in church gatherings in my country, the Philippines. The worship leader shouts out 'God is good!' and the congregation responds, 'All the time!' Even in the midst of the pandemic, when church gatherings are not possible, I continue to hear pastors and worship leaders declaring in their online worship services, 'God is good! All the time!' I even saw a post on social media asking: 'Who is bold enough to say that God is good even in the midst of the pandemic?' Maybe some of you will be the first to say, 'Me! God has been good to me!' But how about those who are having a hard time affirming that statement?

The composer of Psalm 73 admits that he struggled in affirming that God is good. Psalm 73 is attributed to Asaph, one of the worship leaders during the time of David and Solomon. Like many worship leaders today, the psalmist also declared, 'God is good.' And he didn't simply say, 'God is good,' he said: '*Surely* God is good' (verse 1, my emphasis). Take note of the word 'surely'. But, unlike worship leaders today, the psalmist was honest enough to admit that he had a hard time affirming that God is good. In verse 2, he confesses, 'But as for me, my feet had almost slipped.' In the Psalms, for one's feet to slip could mean giving up one's walk with God (Psalm 17:5); turning away from God (Psalm 44:18); or losing one's hope in God's goodness (Psalm 73:2). How did the psalmist come to this point?

Why did the psalmist doubt God's goodness?

The Old Testament scholar, Sigmund Mowinckel, says that the psalmist felt 'resentment' because he saw the prosperity of the wicked (verse 3).[1] The word 'prosperity' comes from the Hebrew term *shalom*. To have *shalom* is to have a life characterized by completeness, soundness, welfare and peace. *Shalom* is the last word in the Aaronic blessing: 'The Lord bless you and keep you . . . and give you peace [*shalom*]' (Numbers 6:24–26). *Shalom* is supposed to be the experience of the righteous. But, in Psalm 73, it's the wicked who seem to be having it. The psalmist observes that: 'They have no struggles; their bodies are healthy and strong' (verse 4). What happens when wicked people don't get punished but experience *shalom* instead? They become boastful: 'Therefore pride is their necklace' (verse 6a). They become abusive because they think they can get away with anything: 'they clothe themselves with violence' (verse 6b). They are no longer afraid of anyone, including God: 'Their mouths lay claim to heaven' (verse 9a). They even taunt God: 'They say, "How would God know? Does the Most High know anything?"' (verse 11).

As I read Psalm 73, I could not help but see its reality in my own country. Like the wicked in Psalm 73 who taunt God, President Duterte (of the Philippines) also said on national television: 'God is stupid.' This was after he cursed Obama and the pope! I also see the violence that the psalmist talked about in verse 6. The night after Duterte was sworn into office, thirty-nine people were killed. This was the start of what he calls his 'war on drugs'. According to some sources, more than 30,000 people have been killed or died in this war. The victims are mostly poor and, tragically, the killings continue even during the lockdown. This comes on top of the already miserable situation of many of our people.

According to one survey, the number of people who experienced hunger during the three-month lockdown doubled. Some people from a nearby poor community were forced to go out to beg for food, violating quarantine laws. They said they would rather die of Covid-19 than hunger. But, instead of helping them, the police arrested some of them. One fish vendor was forced to go out to buy fish to sell. Unfortunately, he forgot to take his quarantine pass and, as a result, he was jailed. Meanwhile a police general, the one who implements the quarantine laws in Metro Manila, held his own birthday party, which violated all lockdown laws, and yet was not penalized. When some complained, the President simply said, 'The law is the law, but leave the general to me.' The general remains the implementer of the quarantine laws in Manila.

God is good, all the time? It's not easy to affirm that when this is what you see around you. The psalmist believed in the justice of God expressed in divine retribution; that the righteous will be blessed but the wicked will perish. We see this justice in Psalm 1:

> Blessed is the one
> > who does not walk in step with the wicked

or stand in the way that sinners take
    or sit in the company of mockers,
but whose delight is in the law of the LORD,
    and who meditates on his law day and night . . .

Not so the wicked!
    They are like chaff
    that the wind blows away.
Therefore the wicked will not stand in the judgment,
    nor sinners in the assembly of the righteous.
(Psalm 1:1–2, 4–5)

But what the psalmist saw around him contradicted this. For while the wicked are prospering, those who are trying to maintain a godly life are suffering. The psalmist tried to keep his heart pure: 'I have kept my heart pure and have washed my hands in innocence' (Psalm 73:13). But, in spite of that, he says, 'All day long I have been afflicted' (verse 14). 'All day long' is an expression which means 'all the time'. While others are shouting, 'God is good! All the time!', the psalmist is saying: 'God is not good to me all the time.'

The psalmist had *tampo* with God

Earlier, in verse 1, he had declared: 'Surely God is good.' Now, in verse 13, he repeats the word, 'surely', but this time in a different tone: 'Surely in vain have I kept my heart pure and have washed my hands in innocence.'

I mentioned that the theologian Mowinckel believes that the psalmist was resentful but he does not explain to whom this resentment is directed. Here, it becomes clear that the psalmist felt resentment towards God.

In Filipino, we would call this *tampo*. There is no exact English translation for *tampo*, even 'resentment' does not capture the richness of the word. *Tampo* refers to the feeling of hurt that comes from a failure by someone very close to you to do or fulfil an expected action. You experience *tampo* only with people you are really close to – your spouse, best friend, brother or sister, daughter or son. You do not experience *tampo* with the mayor, unless you are close to her or him! Feelings of hurt or *tampo* with God therefore can be a good sign. It can be an indication of intimacy with God. If you have never felt *tampo* with God, it could mean that you are not yet that close to him.

However, it does not stop with feeling hurt. *Tampo* has to be dealt with or it becomes bitterness. Bitterness, unchecked, can turn to anger. Anger, if left unprocessed, can turn to wrath. There have been Christians who have felt hurt by God and drifted away. Their feet slipped and they lost their foothold completely. We learn from verse 1 that the psalmist, too, almost slipped.

How did the psalmist deal with his *tampo* with God?

It is interesting that in Psalm 73, the psalmist does not address God directly. In the first part of the psalm, God is talked about in the third person. The psalmist expresses his complaints to his audience, not to God. It takes 16 verses before he finally decides to go into the sanctuary of God (verse 17). This is similar to the way we deal with *tampo* in Filipino culture. The person experiencing *tampo* will try to avoid the other person; he'll stamp his feet or even leave the house. The difference in Psalm 73 is that, eventually, the psalmist enters the sanctuary and deals with his *tampo* with God directly.

What does entering the sanctuary of God mean? The sanctuary is the place where one meets with God. As the psalmist says in Psalm 42:2, 'When can I go and meet with God?', referring to his longing to go to the house of God (see verse 4). And what did the psalmist tell God? What was his prayer? The context of Psalm 73, as well as Psalm 74, gives us some clue. The psalmist asks God why. This question is one of the characteristic cries of the lament. Even though the psalmist did not explicitly ask this, one can sense it in his complaints about the prosperity of the wicked and his own experience of suffering. Yohanna Katanacho's rendering of Psalm 73:1 in his book *Praying through the Psalms* captures the lament of the psalmist: 'O Lord! If you are good, then why don't you remove oppression?'[2] The context of the next psalm – Psalm 74 – confirms the question 'Why?'

One of the developments in biblical interpretation is the idea that the psalms were not randomly placed together. Rather, there is a deliberate and purposeful arrangement. So, for example, that Psalm 73 is followed by Psalm 74 should not be seen as merely accidental or incidental. Like

Psalm 73, Psalm 74 is also attributed to Asaph. A comparison between Psalms 73 and 74 shows important links. They both use the term 'sanctuary' (73:17; 74:7) and 'ruin' (73:18; 74:3). It is not an accident that Psalm 74 begins with the question 'Why?' In English translations, Psalm 74 begins with 'O God': 'O God, why . . . ?' (NIV; ESV); in the Hebrew, the 'Why?' comes first: 'Why, O God?' One commentator thought that the psalmist lacked proper etiquette when he started with the question 'Why?' But the reason Psalm 74 begins in this way is because it is not meant to be read alone. Psalm 74 is intended to be a companion to Psalm 73. According to the commentator Clinton McCann, 'It seems likely that the experience of the "I" [in Psalm 73] is offered as a model to the whole of God's people in dealing with the prosperity of the wicked.'[3]

In Psalm 74 the people not only asked God why, they also uttered what is called an imprecatory prayer. I believe the psalmist also prayed the same way in Psalm 73.

In Filipino, the imprecatory prayer is captured by the word *pagsusumbong*. The idea in *pagsusumbong* is that there is a powerful bully and a victim who is weak and vulnerable, usually a child. The child goes to someone to report what was done to him. Who are the bullies in these psalms? In Psalm 73, they are wicked, powerful and abusive people. In Psalm 74:19, they are described as 'wild beasts': 'Do not hand over the life of your dove to the wild beasts.' Notice how the victim is described in verse 19 as a dove. That is why the community goes to God and says: 'Rise up, O God, and defend your cause' (verse 22). The prayer, 'Rise up', arose out of the context of battle. Whenever Israel would set forth with the ark, they would shout: 'Rise up, O Lord, may your enemies be scattered, may your foes flee before you' (Numbers 10:35–36). Based on this context, we can say that the psalmist in Psalm 73 also prayed an imprecatory prayer against the wicked.

The imprecatory prayers are expressions of trust and hope. As one commentator explains:

> These prayers to God to judge the wicked are an expression of hope in God's justice . . .
>
> By calling on God to intervene the psalmist is affirming that God is the utterly fair and all-knowing judge. To those who are suffering they are a message of hope: God will not let the wicked get away with it forever.[4]

That is why it is not surprising that right after the psalmist entered the sanctuary, he gained assurance: 'Surely you place them on slippery ground; you cast them down to ruin' (Psalm 73:18). The word 'surely' is mentioned for the third time. At the end of his prayer, he uses the word 'good' again. 'But as for me, it is good to be near God. I have made the Sovereign LORD my refuge' (verse 28).

'God is good, all the time?' The psalmist would respond by saying, 'What is really good is to be near God, to encounter him and open one's heart to him, to have someone to go to in the midst of all of life's anguish and torment – that is what is really good.'

This seminar was followed by a Q&A session with Rico Villanueva.

What do you think makes the difference between lamenting and just grumbling?

Grumbling is more of an expression of unbelief or lack of faith, just like we read in the book of Numbers. When the people grumbled, God became angry and judged them because, in spite of all the miracles that God had done, they still did not believe. Lament, on the other hand, is more of an expression of faith. For example, when the psalmist asks God why, he's asking why precisely because he genuinely believes in God's Word. So, for example, like a child would trust in his father or mother's promise, the psalmist believes what God says; that is why he laments when God appears to be not doing what he said or promised. In the talk this morning, in Psalm 73, we also see there that the lament is a sign of intimacy. The closer you are to God, the more open you become with him.

How can we encourage people to lament honestly, but without losing their hope in God?

Lament, in itself, is a sign of hope. You are lamenting because you believe that there is someone with whom you can be honest about what you really think. Of course, some people feel afraid that, if you lament too much, you might lose your faith. But, actually, the more you become open to God and come to him to ask why and pour out your heart, the closer you come to him. Sometimes, after a moment of lament, you receive this hope. That is our experience, after we cry out to God, after we lament, there's some sort of a release. So, actually, the hope arises, sometimes, out of the lament.

Of course, there may be times when lament can take you on a downward spiral, so it's also important that you don't only lament alone. You see, lament in the Bible is not only private but there is a community. Even in the Old Testament, the psalms are used in the liturgy, in the community of God's people. So, you don't lament alone but with the community.

Do you think that wicked oppression by a seeming cabal of despots globally is unique for our time? Why are Christians seen to support them in many countries? It's not unique to our time. We had, of course, Hitler. In my own history, we had the Spaniards for three hundred years. But the problem is: why are Christians supporting them? I think this is where the lack of lament comes in because in the lament you also see the imprecatory prayers. They are the prayers for God's justice. Some Christians only know one kind of prayer: bless, bless, bless. Even when there are wicked people around, they would just say, 'Bless it!' I see that in my own country. But how about if we try the imprecatory prayer? I think the reason why Christians support these leaders is partly because we have neglected the lament and the imprecatory prayers, in particular.

Thank you for enriching God's Word with Filipino cultural perspectives – a great blessing to the worldwide church. Can you explain why, in Western cultures, hardly any Bible teachers will mention imprecation, let alone understand it?

Thank you for your appreciation of my own culture. When I write to explain Psalm 73, I could not but use my own culture because I realize that my own Filipino culture actually helps me understand the psalms better.

One reason I think why, in the Western cultures, they don't teach imprecation that much is probably because that's where they need another culture to help them. For example, I mentioned *pagsusumbong*, which is equivalent in my own culture to 'imprecation'. You know, when there's a bully, you need someone to protect you. That's called *pagsusumbong*. So, you go to this person whom you trust, and that is imprecatory prayer in my own culture, which can also be used by Westerners in understanding this application of the imprecation, I think.

In Psalm 73:15, the psalmist seems to distance himself from the things he'd said earlier. What do you make of that change in the psalm there?

That's a good question but also a difficult one because the psalmist seems to be saying that what he said in the previous verses is wrong: his expressions of doubt; his indirect complaints. But, as I mention in my talk, the psalmist had this resentment or, in the Filipino culture, something we would understand as *tampo*. So, the psalmist is already grumbling against God *but in his heart*. There's the danger of completely slipping away and becoming like the wicked. The psalmist may have been tempted to go that way and almost turn away from God. The main difference is that he went to God, and I think that's the key in the lament.

When you struggle with feelings of resentment, don't own that within you, go to God. Use this to be closer to him. The problem is sometimes Christians are taught not to be brutally honest with God. Some Christians just keep within them their feelings of hurt, which become more serious until it's too late; they have drifted away from God and they have lost their faith. The psalmist is teaching us a way to deal with that: 'I'm struggling with my faith but I will come to God.' So that's what he did in Psalm 73.

Is there a danger, in lament, that we blame God rather than take responsibility, especially for our own sin?
There are times when there's the danger of blaming God, rather than taking responsibility for our sins. But the difference with the lament, though, is that lament arises out of extremely difficult situations, over which you do not have any control. You've done your part. For example, poor people – they're powerless. So, you're lamenting because you've done your part, and you're asking God why, like in Psalm 10:1, 'Why, Lord, do you stand far off? Why do you hide yourself in times of trouble?' So, if you have done your responsibility and yet things are still the same – and you've been praying to God but there seems

to be no answer – then I think that's not blaming God but just being honest to God about what you really feel.

How does lamenting fit with James' call to 'consider it pure joy . . . whenever you face trials' (James 1:2)?

Not only James but even the apostle Paul says, 'Rejoice in the Lord always' (Philippians 4:4). But that does not mean that we will always rejoice. There are also times when the apostle Paul says, 'mourn with those who mourn' (Romans 12:15). In the same way, there will be times when you want to 'count it all joy' but you just can't, you know? The beauty with the lament is it's OK to be not OK, I used this as the title of my book. I mean, 'Lord, honestly, I want to rejoice. I want to count it all joy but I just can't.' Even our Lord, when he was on the cross, didn't count it all joy, he lamented, 'My God, my God, why have you forsaken me?' (Matthew 27:46; Mark 15:34). He was quoting Psalm 22:1.

What difference does the coming of Christ make to how, or even whether, we lament?

With the coming of Christ, we have hope in the Lord and that is why we have more courage to confront our situation, and we can lament. One of the challenges in the lament is to confront our situations. Unfortunately, Christians often tend to deny the situation. Of course, we always *say* that God is in control. But, what if, like the psalmist, you find yourself in a situation that is really tragic? The good thing is that we know that even the tragic has a place in God's divine sovereignty because of Jesus' resurrection.

Some Christians think that because Christ has already come, we should no longer lament, that lament is an Old Testament thing but, as I mentioned, Jesus cried on the cross. By doing that, he did two things: first, he affirmed the lament of the Old Testament people; second, he provided a model for the people of God now – New Testament believers – that it's all right to lament before God.

Notes

1. Sigmund Mowinckel, *Psalms in Israel's Worship*, vol. 2 (Blackwell, 1962), p. 36.
2. Yohanna Katanacho, *Praying through the Psalms* (Langham, 2018), p. 73.
3. Clinton McCann, *A Theological Introduction to the Book of Psalms: The Psalms as Torah* (Abingdon Press, 1993), p. 142.
4. Gordon Wenham, *The Psalter Reclaimed: Praying and Praising with the Psalms* (Crossway, 2013), p. 49.

Evening Celebrations

Why hope? Grace!
(2 Thessalonians 2:13–17)

Mike Cain

Mike Cain came to know Christ through the witness of his best friend at school. After serving churches in London and Leipzig, he became the senior pastor of Emmanuel Bristol (a family of church-planting churches) and a regular speaker at university missions and Bible teaching conferences. He is passionate about persuading people that the gospel is both true and good. He is married to Clare, has two teenage children and is an enthusiastic fisherman, kayaker, tennis player and theatregoer.

Hope is like a holiday. You're worn out, so you book a holiday. The holiday is months away but as soon as it's booked, you start dreaming of the day you can stretch out on the shore of Derwentwater, climb Helvellyn or just take in the view of Buttermere. Having a holiday to look forward to in the future gives you strength to keep going in the present.

Paul is writing to the Thessalonians and to us about the future that we have to look forward to – the Day of the Lord, he calls it; the day when Jesus comes again and deals with all that is wrong in this world and puts everything right. The word that Paul uses to describe it is 'glory'. Jesus' glory is his brilliance. Paul says that when Jesus comes again, we will see him and marvel at his brilliance. He will restore creation to what it was meant to be. We will look at the world made new and we'll see a world without disease, death and sin. We will look at what he has done and say, 'Isn't he brilliant?' Paul also talks of Jesus being glorified in his people (2 Thessalonians 1:10). He will mend our broken hearts; he will fix our broken lives; and he will make us like him. We will look at each other and say, 'Look at what he has done. Isn't he brilliant?'

Waiting for Jesus

In 1 Thessalonians 1:9–10, Paul reminds the believers of how they had turned from idols to serve the living and true God, and to wait for his Son from heaven. The Thessalonians were waiting for Jesus. They were dreaming of the day when Jesus comes back to make all things new. They were looking forward to glory. That's the future that gave them strength to keep going in the present because, right now, they are facing persecutions and trials (2 Thessalonians 1:4). They keep going because they have got the Day of the Lord to look forward to. Right now, we might be crying but we keep going; we keep going because, one day, he will wipe all our tears dry.

Then some people start telling the Thessalonians that the Day of the Lord has already come, that Jesus is not coming back to make all things new, there is nothing to look forward to, this world of trials and tears is as good as it gets. How did you feel when your holiday was cancelled because of Covid-19? It's hard to keep going through the grind of life if there's nothing to look forward to. Friends, we may not have people telling us that the Day of the Lord has been cancelled but maybe, on some level, we've lost confidence that Jesus is coming again, that he's going to deal with all that's wrong, put everything right, wipe away all tears and make all things new. We're not sure if the holiday is coming in the future. When following Jesus costs us, when standing for him means we get hurt, it is hard to keep going. If we're not sure about the future, it seems as if we're on a small boat on a big sea and there is no sign of land.

Jesus will finish what he started

Paul says in 2 Thessalonians 2:1–2, 'we ask you, brothers and sisters, not to become easily unsettled'. He doesn't want us to become unsettled. He doesn't want us to capsize in the Christian life. He's heading to verse 15, where he says, 'So then, brothers and sisters, stand firm.' He wants us to stand firm. So, the first thing he does is insist that the Day of the Lord has not been cancelled. Jesus is coming again. I wonder if you've lost confidence in whether that's really true.

In 1 Thessalonians 1:10, Paul connects the coming again of Jesus to the resurrection of Jesus. He talks about how the Thessalonians are waiting for the Son from heaven, whom the Lord raised from the dead. It's the resurrection that gives us confidence, that shows us this is not all there is, that there is more. The resurrection shows us Jesus is alive, he's King and he's coming back. The point is that he's coming back to finish what he started.

A guy came to fix our boiler. He opened it up, was with us about ten minutes and then went away. He said he had to get some parts. We didn't sit there, wondering if he was going to come back or not. We knew he hadn't just come to open up the boiler. The whole point of his coming was to fix it. He'd started but he'd not finished, so we knew he'd come back. And he did. What the salvation of Jesus came to bring is bigger than we sometimes think. Jesus didn't just come, die, rise and disappear to leave us to it, he came to restore the world to how it was meant to be. You look at his resurrection and you see the beginnings of the new creation but it's very obvious that he's not yet finished. So, will he come back? Yes, because his coming back is not the odd bit tagged on at the end; it's about finishing what he started. He came, which means he *will* come again. We live in a world in which plans change, holidays fall through; the future is very uncertain. But if we are Christians, we have what Paul calls a good hope, a future to look forward to that will not be cancelled. The Day of the Lord is coming. The One who came will come again to finish what he has started, to make all things new. Glory!

Between now and then

What Paul talks about in 2 Thessalonians 2:1–12 is between now and that day. The world will be awash with lies that will deceive people and lead them away from God. Lies that will mean when Jesus comes, instead of being invited into glory, they will be shut out, 'condemned' (verse 12). We have to back up a bit to see what's at stake. The believers were unsettled and Paul settled them: the Day of the Lord is coming. But can you see that, in settling them, Paul might have unsettled them again? The Day of the Lord is coming but, between now and then, if the world is awash with lies, what's to stop us from falling for them? What's to stop our being deceived?

The voices in the papers, every film we see, every song we hear, the voices at school, in college and at work, say, 'How can you be so arrogant as to claim to have the truth? There are lots of different ways of seeing things. It's people like you who cause division and peddle hate. You've just got to let people be true to who they want to be and do what they want to do.' What they say sounds so attractive. I don't want them to think that I'm intolerant or hateful. I want them to like me.

So, the Day of the Lord is coming but I feel as if I'm in a small boat on a very big sea, blown around by a hostile world. There are days when I fear that I'm going to capsize. So, yes, glory is coming; I'm just not sure if I will be part of it because I'm not sure if I can keep going. Do you feel like that?

God has got hold of you for glory

Here's what Paul wants you to know. Yes, the devil is at work in this world but so is God. He is at work in you and he has got hold of you for glory. Look at who the hero is in these verses. Verse 13: 'But we ought always to thank God for you, brothers and sisters.' Why thank God for you? Because the story of your lives is the story of what he is doing. Verse 13: you are 'loved by the Lord, because God chose you'. Verse 14: 'He called you.'

I'm in my small boat on this big sea, and I'm not sure if I can keep going. What Paul is saying is that I can keep going because God has got hold of me for glory. Just take in the medicine of those words: 'loved by the Lord'.

We look down the years ahead and we worry in the face of a hostile world, 'What if my love for him grows cold?' Well, do you see? He's the hero. It's not about your love for him; it's about his love for you. Look at verse 16: 'May our Lord Jesus Christ himself and God our Father, who *loved us'* (my emphasis) – typical Paul: 'loved us' – past tense. Do you want to know how much God loves you? Look back to the cross, look at Jesus. See a love that's prepared to lay down its life for you. People are going to hate you for what you believe. It's going to be really hard but, whatever happens, the Lord loves you. He's never going to stop loving you, and that's because he chose you.

It's a wonderful thing to be chosen, to have someone set their heart on you. Normally, you get chosen because you deserve a place on the team, because you're fast or successful or funny. It makes you feel really good about yourself: 'They chose me!' But what happens when you lose your speed or you're not so successful or you don't make people laugh any more? You get dropped. It's not like that with God.

'God chose you as firstfruits' (2 Thessalonians 2:13) or, if you look at the footnote, 'because from the beginning God chose you'. At the beginning, before we were born, what had we done to deserve our place on God's team? Nothing. Do you see? There you are in your small boat on this big sea, thinking, 'I'm going to blow it! I'm going to mess up and God will drop me.' No, God chose you. He set his heart on you from the beginning. Just as there's nothing you did to deserve it, there's nothing you can do to 'undeserve' it, which means he's never going to drop you.

Do you see why God has loved and chosen us? 'To be saved' (verse 13). It's a contrast with verse 12, which speaks of people who will be condemned because they don't believe the truth. That's what we fear: 'What if that's me?' Paul is reassuring us, saying God chose you not to be condemned but to be *saved* – to be people who do believe the truth. He chose you to be saved through the sanctifying work of the Spirit and through belief in the truth. Even your believing in the truth is the Spirit's work in you.

'Paul, are you sure? Are you sure he's at work in us? Are you sure he's got hold of us?' Paul says, '[Don't you remember?] He called you to this through our gospel' (verse 14). It's language that picks up on what he said to them in 1 Thessalonians 1: 'Don't you remember when we preached the gospel to you? Do you remember how that gospel turned your lives around? You turned from idols to serve the living God, to wait for his Son from heaven.'

There was a time when you didn't care about being ready for the Day of the Lord. But the very fact that, today, you care, that you want to be there shows that something in your heart has changed. God has called you; God has got hold of you. Friends, do you see why he's got hold of you? That you might share in the glory of our Lord Jesus Christ. He's got hold of you so that, when Jesus comes again in glory and the world sees his brilliance, you will not be shut out. You will share in it. People will look at you and marvel at what he has done.

I know that the idea of God choosing us raises all kinds of questions. *But* what a relief it is. We live in a hostile world, awash with lies. By myself, it's very hard for me to keep hold of God but what a relief that he has got hold of me.

The future is guaranteed

Let's see what Paul says in 2 Thessalonians 2:16: our God is the God 'who loved us and by his grace gave us eternal encouragement and good hope'. The good hope that is ours – that holiday that's never going to be cancelled is ours. Why? Because, by his grace, he gave it to us. If glory were something I had to get for myself – not a chance – small boat, big sea, capsize. But the future is guaranteed because glory is a gift he gave to me.

When I was 10, I dreamed of going to Lord's cricket ground to watch a test match. How could I get there? Even if I could afford a ticket, how would I know which train to catch to London? How would I know how to find my way across London on the Underground? The whole idea made me nervous. But that summer, I got to Lord's. In the late August sunshine, I watched a young David Gower make seventy-one dreamy runs against New Zealand. How did I get there? My dad took me. He bought the tickets. He drove us to the station. He got us on the right train. In the Underground, he held my hand. When we got to St John's Wood, he led me through the crowds, into the ground. Then he led me to the stands to find our seats. I remember walking up the steps at the back of the stand in the shade and that magical moment as we stepped out into the light – there was Lord's in all its glory and I was there to share it. Why? Because my dad took me. By myself, I was never going to make it to Lord's. I was never going to get on the right train, find my way round the

Tube and push my way through the crowds, but I got there because Dad took me.

Friends, by ourselves, we're never going to make it to glory. It's a hostile world. It's hard to follow Jesus. There are persecutions and trials, and the world is awash with lies that are so attractive. If it were all down to me, I'd soon lose my way. *But* it isn't all down to me; it isn't all down to you. As my dad got me to Lord's, your Father in heaven has taken you by the hand and he will get you to glory.

'So then, brothers and sisters, stand firm and hold fast to the teachings we passed on to you, whether by word of mouth or by letter' (verse 15). A hostile world says, 'How can you believe this stuff Paul teaches about Jesus? Do you really believe he's coming back to judge the world? Do you really believe this stuff about how God wants people to live?' It's so tempting to walk away, isn't it? Especially when it costs us; especially when they hate us for it. It makes my heart ache. It makes for tears. If there is no glory to come – forget it. I'll turn back. I'll just go along with everyone else; just go along with the crowd. *But* what we've seen in these verses is that there *is* glory to come. Jesus is coming back to finish what he started, to make all things new, and we *are* going to be there. Why can we be so certain? Because it's not just me in my small boat on this big sea, awash with lies. God has got hold of us.

That 10-year-old me is half-way to Lord's, on my own. At the first sign of getting lost, the first time I feel afraid of the crowds, I turn back. But if Dad has got hold of me,

I'm not going to turn back. There are moments when I might panic and feel anxious but I'm not turning back because my dad is taking me to Lord's. Friends, we're afraid of the crowds: what they say to us, what they do to us; the lies they tell. It is so tempting to turn back. *But* we're not going to turn back. Why would we when God our Father is taking us to glory? There will be a day when we step out into the light of a world made new and marvel at what he has done, his brilliance, and that we can share in it. So, stand firm – but it's hard.

Paul concludes, 'May our Lord Jesus Christ himself and God our Father, who loved us and by his grace gave us eternal encouragement and good hope, encourage your hearts and strengthen you in every good deed and word' (verses 16–17). Do you see what Paul prays? It's not just that glory is a gift given to us (that the Lord has left tickets by the gate for us to collect), the point is that he is with us along the way. When we're in trials and tears, he's got us by the hand. Paul is praying that we would know the reality of that, that we would know we can keep going because Jesus Christ himself and God our Father are giving us the strength to keep going.

How Can I Hope? New Birth!
(1 Peter 1:3–5, 22–25)

Andy Prime

Andy is married to Sarah, and they have a son called Reuben and a dog called Sanka. He is a graduate from Oak Hill College and was an associate pastor at Charlotte Chapel, Edinburgh. In 2014, he left Charlotte Chapel to join 20schemes and, in 2017, planted a church in Gracemount, a housing scheme in Edinburgh.

OK, I've got twenty minutes! I want to use this time for a thought experiment. Imagine right now, at the start of our twenty minutes, you compose an email to everyone in your contacts list; you also post it as a status on Facebook to all your friends. You send a tweet to all your followers; you ping this round all your colleagues at work; and you forward it to all your family in a WhatsApp group. And this is the message:

> I believe in God as the Creator of everything. I believe in the Bible as God's authority on everything. I believe in hell as the deserved destiny of everyone. I believe in Jesus as the only one who is able to save anyone. And, because of those things, I believe that the Bible's teaching on gender, sexuality, marriage and family are not just right but they're good.

That's it: that's the tweet; that's the email; that's the post.

How do you feel, as your finger hovers over the send button? Hitting the send button on that could feel a little bit like dropping a grenade. But imagine you post it now, at the start of this twenty minutes, and you put your phone away for the rest of that time. What notifications do you reckon you'll have back when you check in? Now, if all you've got back is fan mail – amens, hallelujahs, high fives – then you've obviously got no non-Christian friends because, if you throw that into the public square in the UK in 2020, you'll be thrown into the lion's den on social media. You'll be abused (1 Peter 4:4); you'll be accused;

you'll be hated by people who call you a 'hater'; or, to use the language of 1 Peter 1:1, you'll feel like an exile. Peter is writing to the homeless and to the hated.

Mainstream Christianity is considered to be a polluted backwater by mainstream culture. Jesus was clear on this: 'You follow me and you'll be hated by the world' (see John 15:18–19). Increasingly today, all over the world, if you become a Christian, it will make your life on earth harder. The invitation to become a Christian is not an invitation to join the comfort of a country club; it's an invitation to enter the contempt of a concentration camp. You could legitimately object at this point and say, 'Isn't Virtually Keswick meant to be about hope? Did this lad not get the memo? He's talking about "hate", not "hope".' But this hatred towards Christians is why Peter penned a letter rammed with hope for Christians; that's why he writes at the end, 'I have written to you briefly, encouraging you and testifying that this is the true grace of God. Stand fast in it' (1 Peter 5:12). Peter gets that it's going to be massively tempting for Christians to slip back in and drift with the flow. That's why he's got to write to you and to me, 'Stand fast.'

Standing fast in the heat and the hate takes heaps of hope. Peter knows this; he's lived it. Hope will be the difference between caving in to a slave girl in the hearing of a Jerusalem cockerel or standing up to be crucified upside down in front of Roman centurions. Hope transformed Peter and made him stand fast where he once slipped. Hope can and *must* transform us, and this hope needs to be huge because hate can be loud. So here it is, here is the hope: 'Praise be to the God and Father of our Lord Jesus Christ! In his great mercy he has given us new birth into a living hope' (1 Peter 1:3).

Here's what Peter's saying: the antidote, the corrective to your pandering to the world is praising God for the hope he's given you in Jesus. The way to stand fast and not slip back is to marvel at the massiveness of the mercy of God. As he works through it, the reason for the praising, the greatness and the mercy – the content of the gift – is summed up in this picture: new birth. And Peter milks that image twice: in verses 3 and 23. For him, the phrase 'new birth' becomes like a womb. All of our hope in Jesus is contained in, and comes from, this womb of new birth.

To understand the phrase, we need to appreciate our first birth, our old birth, and Peter helps us with that. Look at 1 Peter 1:18–19: 'For you know that it was not with perishable things such as silver or gold that you were redeemed from the empty way of life handed down to you from your ancestors, but with the precious blood of Christ.' Here is the inheritance that is handed down between generations of humanity. It's an inheritance of emptiness. As soon as I was out of my mother's womb, I entered into an empty existence, without God and without hope. From an earthly perspective, some of us will inherit a fortune from our ancestors; some of us will inherit only debt. But *all of us* get handed down this empty way of life. It's empty, partly, because it's so temporary. Everything perishes, spoils and fades.

At the end of chapter 1 verse 24, Peter says life is like a flower. You might hear that and think, 'Aww, that's nice. I'm a flower: I must be beautiful, pretty and smell gorgeous.' Wrong. The flower illustration is not to say you're beautiful and pretty but to say that you will wither and die. It's this emptiness, that my forefathers handed down to me, which my heavenly Father lifts me out of. He lifts me out of it through what? The gift of new birth. It's the perfect image for Peter to choose. He doesn't choose it; he nicks it from Jesus in John 3. But it's perfect because it shows, first, the massiveness of God's mercy.

The massiveness of mercy

Just as emptiness can't produce fullness, nothing can't conjure up something. Withering death can't produce imperishable life. Children can't birth themselves. So too, God's mercy to us in giving us new birth is not something we produce ourselves. It's something God gifts us. Hope comes from God. In my first birth, my physical birth, I'm birthed by my earthly mother. But in my new birth, my spiritual birth, I'm birthed by my heavenly Father. My first birth sees me sharing a likeness with my blood family because I'm stained by the guilt of my disobedience. My new birth from my heavenly Father sees those stains removed as I'm sprinkled with the blood of Jesus for the obedience of faith. My first birth enslaves me to an inheritance of emptiness. My new birth redeems me to an inheritance of imperishable, unfading life. My first birth propels me, withering, towards the grave. My new birth propels me towards living hope, through an empty grave. You see, we praise God because our hope comes from him, because that new birth magnifies the massiveness of his mercy.

The totality of the transformation

New birth is also a perfect image to show the totality of the transformation. Our birth is the most fundamentally transformative moment in our lives. It doesn't get more momentous than moving from unborn to born; it's unrepeatable. *And* the transformation in a Christian is as fundamental, as momentous as birth. It's not just like the adding of a hobby, it is the renewal of the whole. It's transformation from emptiness to hopefulness, from withering death to forever life, partly because it comes from an everlasting and ever-living Father. But it comes also through the resurrection of Jesus Christ from the dead (1 Peter 1:3). Here's the scoop: at the resurrection, Jesus' tomb becomes a womb – a womb that produces new life. After the pronouncement of his death at his crucifixion came the announcement of life in his resurrection. And here's the transformation the risen Jesus achieves: the empty tomb means that death is not the end. The empty tomb means that life is not empty. The empty tomb means that the first you – the empty you, the withering you – doesn't need to be the last you.

If you're not a Christian, maybe you have become re-signed to emptiness. Later on, in chapter 4, Peter makes a connection: Jesus' being the one who brought life from death makes him the one who will judge the living and the dead. If you think about it, his resurrection and his final judgment remove emptiness from our existence. They give meaning to everything. There's a seriousness to that, but in the seriousness you see the sweetness. Jesus' life isn't empty. Death doesn't render everything vanity. His life after death can produce life after death in you. You become something you weren't before: full of everlasting life; full of never-dying hope. That's the transformation – new birth. From everlasting Father, through the ever-living Son, creating a new you, a living-with-hope you. We praise God because we're not what we once were.

And, by the way, if you are a Christian, that change in you that gives you heavy hope is the same change that will invite hatred. Peter explains:

> For you have spent enough time in the past doing what
> pagans choose to do – living in debauchery, lust,
> drunkenness, orgies, carousing and detestable idolatry.
> They [the world] are surprised that you do not join them
> in their reckless, wild living, and they heap abuse on you.
> (1 Peter 4:3–4)

It's the change that's happened in you that invites the criticism of you. Think of it this way: if all Jesus had to offer you was for this life, then it's not worth standing up for him at school; it's not worth living for him in the office; it's not worth making him known everywhere because it just makes your life a whole lot harder. *But* if his resurrection does transform emptiness to hope and the temporary to the eternal, then it changes the way you look at suffering for Jesus.

Look at the way Peter sees it: 'In all this you greatly rejoice, though now for *a little while* you may have had to suffer grief in all kinds of trials' (1 Peter 1:6; my emphasis). If you lose sight of the living hope, then suffering for being a Christian will feel like for ever and it won't be worth it. But if you stand fast in this living hope, suffering for being a Christian will seem like a little while and totally worth it. The living hope transforms suffering to a little while.

We also need this living hope when we catch ourselves envying the world. When standing fast is excruciating, sliding back appeals because it looks easy. We need to stop, though, and each ask ourselves the question, 'What am I envying?' We're envying emptiness. When we walk away from Jesus, we're walking away to nothing. Peter reminds us, our faith is 'of greater worth than gold' (1 Peter 1:7).

So, stand fast; the resurrection is not a dream. The tomb is empty; your hope can be full. New birth is the perfect picture of the massiveness of God's mercy and the totality of the transformation.

Third, new birth is a kind of womb that shows the hope of home.

Hope of home

Peter called this group of Christians 'exiles' (verse 1). Getting a battering for Jesus has led to a scattering. They've fled home and become homeless. So, from one angle, you can read that word 'exile' as a dreary word. It speaks of their past suffering. But, for Peter, that word is given a fresh lick of paint by the transformation we've just talked about. It's not a word that speaks of their lack of an earthly home; it's a word that speaks of their hope of an eternal home. They lost their earthly inheritance when they had to flee their homes for following Jesus. They lost houses, land, possessions; they lost everything that can perish, spoil or fade. But, in following Jesus, they have gained an inheritance – one that can never perish, spoil or fade.

Again, think of Peter who is writing this: he had left everything to follow Jesus. He'd left his living when he'd walked away from his nets; he'd left his family; he'd left his home when he walked away from Galilee. In time, he was going to lose his life, murdered for following and preaching Jesus. He probably had very little when he died. But, because of the gift of new birth from his heavenly Father, he was being kept for his Father's inheritance. His hope in life and death – the new birth that gives living hope – was the hope of home.

To be an exile as a Christian is not to be *homeless*; it's to be *hopeful*. Yes, they're away from home but they're going home. This world may be a concentration camp for

Christians but Christ is going to bring them to a celestial city. The empty tomb of Jesus' resurrection is not just a womb that gives birth to new life in a Christian but it promises the restoration of all things. Our hope of home is kept for us in heaven (verse 4) but heaven is not that home. Home will be new lives in new bodies, in a new creation, when Christ is revealed. See, our new birth is coupled to the new creation; our being born again is bonded to his coming again. So, we praise God because he'll bring us safe home.

New birth, the massiveness of mercy; new birth, the totality of the transformation; and new birth, the hope of home.

So, twenty minutes are up, give or take. You pick up your phone and you check the notifications. Perhaps you've been unfriended and you've been heaped with abuse. Maybe you've been unfollowed, lost your job or been removed from WhatsApp groups. Perhaps you've been disowned by family, ridiculed publicly or dismissed as a radical. Maybe worse? Now, you've got two options. You can consider the heat and the hate too much; you can slide back into the easiness of drifting downstream into mainstream emptiness. The calculation there is that the grave is the end, the resurrection is a myth, hell isn't real and the fading glory of this world is all there is. *Or* you can stand fast by setting your gaze on all the reasons to praise God – great mercy, living in hope, the risen Jesus and unfading inheritance. The calculation there is that the empty tomb is the womb that gifts you new birth – and that this Word of God endures for ever. So,

> Be alert and of sober mind. Your enemy the devil prowls around like a roaring lion looking for someone to devour. Resist him, standing firm in the faith, because you know that the family of believers throughout the world is undergoing the same kind of sufferings.
>
> And the God of all grace, who called you to his eternal glory in Christ, after you have suffered a little while, will himself restore you and make you strong, firm and steadfast. To him be the power for ever and ever. Amen.
> (1 Peter 5:8–11)

How Can I Hope? The Scriptures!
(Romans 15:1–13)

Amy Orr-Ewing

Dr Amy Orr-Ewing is a senior vice president with Ravi Zacharias International Ministries (RZIM) and Co-director of the Oxford Centre for Christian Apologetics (OCCA). She leads a team of pioneering apologist-evangelists and speaks around the world on how the Christian faith answers the deepest questions of life. Amy is married to Frog and helps to lead Latimer Minster, a church plant and community on a farm in Buckinghamshire. She and Frog have three children.

During the lockdown, my teenagers have been regularly extolling the merits of various fast foods. We've had Nando's, McDonald's and KFC described with great detail, as they look forward to the longed-for day when they might, once again, taste the delights of their favourite fast food. For weeks, they've been checking the news – when is McDonald's going to open? Anticipating it with pleasure, expectation and confidence that, one day soon, they're going to be able to bite into that Nando's chicken-wing roulette or that Big Mac. It was a source of delight and encouragement to them to look forward with anticipation.

What are you looking forward to as a Christian? What are you putting your hope, your expectation, your anticipation in? Hope is desperately needed in our culture, as we face such uncertain times. Our jobs, churches and communities have been massively impacted by the pandemic and subsequent lockdown. But is there Christian hope that is more than a vague sense of positive thinking that one day things are going to get better? Is there something more than that kind of positive-thinking sentimentality? Are there any certain or secure anchors for Christian hope?

Endurance and encouragement

In the book of Romans, Paul writes: 'For everything that was written in the past was written to teach us, so that through the endurance taught in the Scriptures and the encouragement they provide we might have hope' (Romans 15:4). In other words, the Scriptures are a secure anchor of confidence that Christian hope is solid – that it's substantial and real, that what was written down in the past was done so carefully, that it can be trusted, that it's not some sort of religious mythology thrown together in a haphazard way. The Bible is, in fact, the most scrutinized and challenged book that the world has ever known. Yet, time and time again, its accuracy and its integrity are upheld by those who examine it.

Luke writes:

> In the fifteenth year of the reign of Tiberius Caesar –
> when Pontius Pilate was governor of Judea, Herod
> tetrarch of Galilee, his brother Philip tetrarch of Iturea
> and Traconitis, and Lysanias tetrarch of Abilene – during
> the high-priesthood of Annas and Caiaphas, the word of
> God came to John son of Zechariah in the wilderness.
> (Luke 3:1–2)

In other words, Luke places his writing firmly in history. He's specific. We know that the fifteenth year of Tiberius was AD 27. It was once said that Lysanias of Abilene was executed by Mark Anthony in 34 BC. Those scholars who noticed that said Luke must have got this wrong – he's mentioning someone who did exist but he's locating him in the wrong time period. Fascinatingly, more recently, this has been shown to be wrong. Inscriptions have been found of a later Lysanias, who was tetrarch of Abilene, and he reigned exactly when Luke said he did. Ancient historians, such as Eduard Meyer, consider Luke to be a first-class historian because his attention to detail has been underscored time and time again. You see, the Scriptures are historically trustworthy; that's a tiny example from Luke's Gospel.

Here in Romans, Paul shares that the endurance taught in the Scriptures and the encouragement they provide actually produce hope in the heart of the believer, and, because the Scriptures can be trusted, that hope is solid. By digging into the Bible, into Scriptures written down for us in the past, we can exercise that muscle of Christian hope, through learning the endurance that they teach and through the encouragement they impart to us.

Ravi Zacharias, my late boss, shared that, when he was ministering in Vietnam in 1971, he had an interpreter who was called Hien Pham. This man worked with him as a translator and had worked with the American forces. Hien travelled with Ravi up and down the countryside, ministering with him, and they became very close. At the end of that trip, Ravi didn't know if their paths would ever cross again but, seventeen years later, he received a phone call from Hien. Ravi said that he immediately recognized his voice. Hien told Ravi his story.

He said that, shortly after Vietnam fell, he was imprisoned on accusations of helping the Americans. His jailers tried to indoctrinate him against democracy and against Christianity. He was forced to read communist propaganda in French and Vietnamese. The daily deluge of Marx and Engels began to take its toll on the man. Hien thought, 'Maybe I've been lied to. Maybe God doesn't exist. Maybe the West has deceived me.' So, he decided, when he woke up the next day, he wasn't going to pray again or think about his faith.

That morning, in the camp, he was assigned the dreaded chore of cleaning the prison latrines. As he cleaned out a tin can overflowing with toilet paper, his eye caught what seemed to be English written on the page. He grabbed it, washed it and, after his cellmates had gone to sleep that night, retrieved the paper and read the words, 'Romans 8'. Trembling, he began to read:

And we know that in all things God works for the good of those who love him, who have been called according to his purpose . . . For I am convinced that neither death nor life, neither angels nor demons, neither the present nor the future, nor any powers, neither height nor depth, nor anything else in all creation, will be able to separate us from the love of God that is in Christ Jesus our Lord.
(Romans 8:28, 38–39)

Hien wept because he knew his Bible and he knew there was no more relevant passage for someone on the verge of giving up. He cried out to God, asking for forgiveness. This was supposed to have been the first day that he wouldn't start his day in prayer but, evidently, God had other plans. As it was, there was an official in the camp who was using a Bible as toilet paper, so Hien asked the commander if he could clean the latrines regularly. Every day, he got another portion of Scripture, cleaned it off and added it to his collection of nightly reading.

When the day came, through an equally providential set of circumstances, for Hien to be released from prison, he started to make plans to leave Vietnam. He began to construct a boat so that he and fifty-three other people could escape. Everything was going well until, a couple of days before their departure, four Vietcong knocked on Hien's door and said that they'd heard he was trying to escape. He denied it and they left. He felt quite relieved but, at the same time, a little bit disappointed with himself. He got down on his knees and he made a promise to God that, if they came back, he would tell them the truth. Within a few hours of when they were due to sail, the Vietcong returned and questioned him, and Hien confessed the truth. To his astonishment, the Vietcong leaned forward and, in hushed tones, asked if they could come along, too.

In an utterly amazing escape plan, fifty-eight people found themselves on the high seas, engulfed by a violent storm. Hien cried out to God: 'Did you bring us here to die?' He said on the phone to Ravi: 'Brother Ravi, if it were not for the sailing ability of those four Vietcong, we would not have made it.' Hien arrived safely in Thailand and now lives in America.

What are you looking forward to? What is the basis of your hope? Here, Paul tells us to turn to the Scriptures and learn the endurance of the Lord Jesus, and receive the encouragement from his Word that we need. Don't give up on God. Don't dismiss hope as wishful thinking. Biblical hope is rooted in reality and in the truth of the Bible, and that cannot be shaken. Receive the encouragement of God's Word right now, just as Hien Pham did, that nothing can separate you from the love of God that is in Christ Jesus.

Unity and mission

Hope is rooted in Scripture. Then we see in Romans 15:5–9 that the overflow of that is unity and mission:

> May the God who gives endurance and encouragement give you the same attitude of mind toward each other that Christ Jesus had, so that with one mind and one voice you may glorify the God and Father of our Lord Jesus Christ.
>
> Accept one another, then, just as Christ accepted you, in order to bring praise to God. For I tell you that Christ has become a servant of the Jews on behalf of God's truth, so that the promises made to the patriarchs might be confirmed and, moreover, that the Gentiles might glorify God for his mercy.

Paul goes on to quote from the Old Testament text of Scripture, speaking of how the Gentiles and all people will extol God, and how the root of Jesse will spring up to rule over the nations and, in Jesus, the Gentiles will hope.

God gives endurance and encouragement through the Scriptures, and the outflow of that will be unity. He will give you the same attitude of mind towards one another that Jesus had, says Paul, 'so that with one mind and one voice you may glorify . . . God' (verse 6). Unity with other Christians is a fruit of this hope and encouragement. How much evidence of hope is there in your life and mine? The one-mind and one-voice unity – how's that coming along?

Paul goes on to emphasize that Jesus came as a Jew, so that the promise to Abraham might be fulfilled – that's the promise of being a blessing to all nations and a light to the Gentiles. The presenting issue of disunity in the Roman church was between Jew and Gentile. For us, racial tensions may be different but the fundamental truth that Christ came for all nations, all people, is powerful and countercultural as much today as it ever has been, and it is under siege.

This truth is under siege from the intersectionality culture warriors, who see Christianity as the lifeblood of colonialism and empire. Yet Christ came that the Gentiles might glorify God, since all are equal, all are image-bearers of God, all are loved by him. This truth that Christ came for all is also under siege from pluralists, who tell us that all views and all paths to God are the same, and that no one can make an exclusive truth claim, all the while stating that pluralism is exclusively true. Yet Christ came that the Gentiles might glorify God. This truth is under siege from the white supremacists who claim Christ is the icon of whiteness for a so-called Christian nation. Yet Christ came that all Gentiles might glorify God. This truth is also under fire from the progressives with their vision of self-improvement and self-realization, their myth of continual human progress. Yet Christ came that all Gentiles might glorify God. He needed to come because we cannot save ourselves.

Do you feel weary of the scandals, the confusions and disunities in the church? Look to Christ in the Scriptures, says Paul, and receive encouragement and hope today. His truth is trustworthy and real. Intersectionality, pluralism, white supremacy, self-realization – they all leave us hopeless, in self-loathing and in division. It is Christ and Christ alone who can save us. Look to him for hope.

Joy and peace

Read the Scriptures and receive his encouragement and his strengthening. The passage says that this will lead to overflow: 'May the God of hope fill you with all joy and peace as you trust in him, so that you may overflow with hope by the power of the Holy Spirit' (Romans 15:13). Hope is God's; he is the God of hope. He is the one who can fill us with hope and hope's bedfellows – joy and peace. Trust in him, receive from him – the promise is real. You and I can overflow with hope by the power of the Holy Spirit.

What might it look like to overflow with hope? One example of what that might look like comes from northern Nigeria. A dear Nigerian friend of mine is a Christian worker there. He has seen many, many people come to Christ, including those from Muslim backgrounds. He told the story of one friend who had come to know Jesus and had decided to stay within the mosque community to reach others with the gospel.

One day my friend received a call from this man, who had been undercover in the mosque, sharing Christ with his Muslim family and friends. The man revealed that his cover had been blown and that he was in a house, surrounded by militants, who had come there with machetes and guns to kill him. He was phoning my friend as he and his wife were lying down hiding on the floor of that house.

My friend described his feeling of responsibility for this Christian brother and sister. He was overwhelmed by the loss that he knew was coming – this man was going to die for his faith. He got into his car to drive his children to school, but he was just so desperate to get to his friend that he headed straight there. As they were driving down the track towards the house, where the man and his wife were, my friend realized that the crowd of militants, who had almost certainly killed his friend, were now walking towards his car.

My friend is ordained; he was wearing a dog collar. Immediately, instinctively, he took off the dog collar and turned down the Christian worship music on his radio. From the back of the car, his 12-year-old son piped up and said, 'Daddy, don't you want them to know we're Christians?' My friend felt very convicted. As a family, they'd made a decision that if they were ever asked to deny Christ at gunpoint, they would not give up their faith. And here was his son asking, 'Daddy, don't you want them to know we're Christians?'

Encouraged by that word, he put the dog collar back on, turned the Christian music back up and began to drive. The crowd parted as they drove through, and everybody looked into the car. My friend thought, 'This is it. My children and I are going to die.' But the crowd just parted and they kept driving. They drove up to the house and walked inside to find that the man and his wife had, in fact, survived. My friend looked at his son, looked at his children, and they experienced the joy and peace of putting their hope in God, even when their lives were most likely at an end. They rejoiced together and worshipped the God of hope and truth.

What does overflowing with hope look like? It's about God and so it necessarily transcends circumstances. Hope is not about whether the answer to prayer happens or not: 'If you answer my prayer, then I'll overflow with hope and trust.' No, this is God's hope, filling us with joy and peace that only he can impart.

Can you trust him with the situations in your life? Can you truly trust him, whatever the outcome – that he is the one who can impart hope into your heart and give you the joy and peace that the Scriptures promise here?

How can I hope? As we dig into the Scriptures, knowing with confidence that there's a reliability and an authenticity there, we can learn the endurance they teach and receive the encouragement we need. How can we hope? We can begin to see a flow of unity and mission, as we trust in

Christ and read the Scriptures. How can we hope? We can receive that overflow: 'May the God of hope fill you with all joy and peace as you trust in him, so that you may overflow with hope by the power of the Holy Spirit' (Romans 15:13).

Our Hope: The Appearing of Jesus Christ (Titus 2:11–14)

Graham Daniels

Graham is married to Michelle, and they have three children and three grandchildren. He is the General Director of Christians in Sport. Graham lives in Cambridge, where he is an associate staff member of St Andrew the Great and a director of Cambridge United Football Club.

Simon was 32 years of age. He'd been a footballer since he was 16 and he thought he'd been a Christian since he was 15. It was a pretty new club; he'd been there a little while, and they were on their way to a game on the team bus. A discussion began about religion. He jumped in, thinking, 'Oh, this is good! I like this conversation,' and he started defending the Christian faith.

Then somebody turned to him and said, 'Hey, Simon. What are you batting for the religious side for?'

He said, 'Cos I'm a Christian,' and he was really earnest.

Somebody laughed at him, but they didn't laugh to make fun of Christianity; it was much worse. It hurt – they laughed that *he* could claim to be a Christian.

He said, 'Why? What are you laughing for?'

And the person said, 'Not the way you live! You can't be a Christian!'

He was mortified.

And here's the thing, he should have been mortified, according to Titus 2. Paul says that Christians should live in such a way 'that no one will malign the word of God' (Titus 2:5). People were maligning the Word of God because of Simon.

Here's the context: Paul writes to Titus and sends him to the island of Crete because there were a lot of people in Crete who were like Simon. They were not taking the Christian message and turning it into some kind of coherent lifestyle that fitted the wonder of the gospel. So, Paul asked Titus to go to Crete, teach the truth of

Christianity so that it changed lives properly, and then to find the right people to lead churches.

Now, you might say, 'What's that got to do with me?' Well, I think, two things:

1. If you say, 'I'm a Christian,' the question is, 'Are you sure that the way you live prevents others maligning the Word of God?'
2. If you're not a Christian, perhaps you're thinking, 'What would it look like for me to be a Christian in such a way that people see Christianity alive and good, not ugly?'

The priority of godliness

This is about the priority of godliness. At the very start of this letter, in the first line, Paul drives this message home by saying he wants the people in Crete to grow in faith by the knowledge of the truth (Titus 1:1). He wants them to know the gospel of Jesus in such a way that it leads to godliness. Knowledge of the truth leads to godliness. Paul says that Titus 'must teach what is appropriate to sound doctrine' (Titus 2:1). If you teach the truth – the sound doctrine – properly, appropriate behaviour should follow. There shouldn't be Simons all over Crete, Simons out in Cambridge or Simons where you live. How do we fix it? That's what we're going to explore.

The practice of godliness

In Titus 2:2–10, Paul turns to the practice of godliness. In these verses, he highlights five particular groups of people: older men, younger men, older women, younger women and people in their workplaces. He talks very specifically about what godliness would look like for each of these groups of people. He lists what people should look like if Christ lives in them. And his summary is that, in every way, their lives should make 'the teaching about God our Saviour attractive' (verse 10). The practice of Christian living should translate into a life of which people say, 'I like what I see. I like her standards. I like her ethics. I like her behaviour. I like her manner. I like her ways. I like her selflessness.'

The power of godliness

You might be thinking, 'I fail all the time! I know the Christian message but if you lived inside me, next door to me or with me, you'd see all my failures.' Hey! Paul isn't talking about the power of *perfection*; he's talking, in verses 11–14, about the power of *godliness*. What does it look like to let the Christian message change you from the inside out? That's what we're going to spend the rest of the time looking at, as Titus is ensuring coherence between Christian teaching and lifestyle.

I want to take you back to Simon. Simon is now a football coach. He's been involved in professional football his whole life. If Simon were here now, he'd say:

To understand the power of godliness, come with me. Come to the field with me. On the field, you need 360-degree vision. What's behind you? What's going on in the defence? What's going on in my own half? What's going on in the attacking half? What can I see? Where's the ball? Where are the people? What's the shape of the game? Only when you can see what's behind, around and up front, can you know where you stand and how to get on with the game.

Sorry if you don't like sport, but you can see the picture, can't you? With that image in mind, how does the power of godliness work?

Look back

Three things. Here's the first – look back. Verse 11: 'For the grace of God has appeared that offers salvation to all people.' Here's the first of three things that must be taught about Christianity if it is to lead to an authentically godly life, transformed by Jesus, even though we're not perfect. Christ has appeared in the past. What did he appear to do? To offer salvation to all people. Jesus Christ, the Son of God died on a cross to take the punishment for my rebellion against God. He died on my behalf. He crashed through the grave. He made me clean; he made me right with God. He paid the price I should pay. He liberated me from my bondage to enmity against God. All this happened at Calvary.

This is the foundation of the Christian message. This is the truth that Titus needs to teach in Crete, the truth that

I need to teach today, and that you and I need to hear. It 'offers salvation' – do you see it in verse 11? – 'to all people'. Don't you love it? Not *some* people. Not just the right type of people. *All* people. Never negotiate for where the grace of God can go. Don't think, '*She* can't become a Christian!' If we look back to the cross, we've got some bearings in history.

Look forwards

We're back on the field. We're looking which way to go now. Look forwards. If we look back to the beginning of our salvation at Calvary, we look forward to when it is perfected, when grace in the future (as well as grace in the past) becomes a reality. Verse 13: 'we wait for the blessed hope – the appearing of the glory of our great God and Saviour Jesus Christ'. Jesus is coming back. The Jesus who died – who appeared, lived and died; who smashed death on our behalf and sent his Spirit to live in us. He'll be back.

Who are you? Where do you come from? Where are you going? The revolution that is the Christian gospel answers these questions and gives us our bearings in life. Once you come to understand this gospel and once you know the free gift of grace from Jesus Christ and his Spirit in your heart, you have a vision for the future. Look at Jesus' vision for our future: 'our great God and Saviour, Jesus Christ, who gave himself for us to redeem us from all wickedness' (verses 13–14). When he died on the cross, Jesus paid the penalty for our wickedness. He said, 'You're free, man! You're free, woman! I've freed you from slavery to wickedness. I've freed you to live. I live in you now.' Christ gave us a vision of a redemption from the slavery of sin. He set us free from those terrible, selfish, hopeless things that we despair about in ourselves. He comes to live in us and says, 'There's a better way. Live it.'

Christ redeems 'us from all wickedness' – but Paul can't stop there, he drives the message home – 'and to purify for himself a people that are his very own' (verse 14). We've been redeemed. We've been rescued from wickedness at Calvary. That's where I've come from; where am I going? I'm going to be a guy who is totally free from sin. It'll never, ever trouble me when Jesus returns. What a hope is mine! Meanwhile, Jesus wants to purify me; he wants to live in me; he wants my focus to be on that day. But still Paul doesn't stop, Jesus wants to 'purify for himself a people that are his very own' (verse 14). I'm his! He died for me! He pays the price; he sets me free. He'll come back. He's at work purifying me. I'm his; he's mine. That's who I am.

The last clause of verse 14 says Jesus wants people who are purified and *'eager* to do what is good' (my emphasis). Don't sit around saying, 'I'm a Christian. I believe he died for me. I believe he beat death. I believe his Spirit lives in me. I believe I'm going to see him one day.' That's not enough! We need to be 'eager to do what is good'. We are to change the world by the power of Jesus – that's the brilliant hope of the Christian. Change the world in Crete, in Cambridge, in the world of sport, wherever you are.

Present grace

We've looked back: we know the past; we know the truths of the gospel. We've looked forwards and have a certain hope for the future that we will meet Christ and he will be thrilled with the vision that we worked out in this life. Now, present grace.

It is God's grace that 'teaches us to say "No" to ungodliness and worldly passions, and to live self-controlled, upright and godly lives in this present age' (verse 12). When I'm confronted with ungodliness, I say, 'I can't live in such a way. Christ has rescued me and liberated me. He has given his life for me. He lives in me and I'm going to choose to live Christ's way.' What is his plan for when I die or when he comes back? It's that he'll embrace me and say, 'Graham, good man. I lived in you. My grace purified you. You collaborated; you allowed me to work in you. You were *eager* to work out the plan I had for you. Come here, my son.' Once you look 360 degrees around life like that, you realize that the gospel transforms the life of a human being for the glory of God. It has to work that way once the gospel is crystal clear.

The power for godliness is the gospel. That's why, at Keswick, we teach the gospel – the historic, wonderful gospel of Christ, as revealed in Scripture. We know it saves us, it prepares us for the future and it gives us a vision for life. We are *eager* to live for Christ and, by his power, we say 'no' to ungodliness and 'yes' to the things of Christ. That's who we are. That's what we're for.

I can't go without finishing the story about Simon. He was so despairing that people laughed at him because he claimed to be, and thought he was, a Christian. There was such a gap between what he understood about Christianity and his lifestyle that he tried to think of anyone he knew who was a Christian. He remembered one guy who had sold him his pension as a young professional footballer. Whenever anyone talked about this guy, they said he was a Christian and he was deeply respected for his integrity. So, he tracked down the guy's number, phoned him up and told him the story: 'I tried to talk about Christianity. I think I'm a Christian. They laughed because of the way I live. What do I do?'

The man said to him, 'I know somebody in your city. I'll introduce you. You two have a chat. He'll explain the Christian gospel to you.'

At 32 years of age, Simon heard the Christian gospel clearly for the first time in his life: what Christ had done for him; how Christ had paid his penalty; how Christ had liberated him and set him free; and how Christ would return for him one day. He learned what that meant for a vision for life now – to live in a way where Christ was at the centre, transforming his life in football. He says he was converted to Christ in those couple of weeks.

Now let me tell you what happened in the middle of lockdown. Week one: a whole bunch of professional footballers came to an online Zoom meeting because no one was at work. Many had never met one another, so people introduced themselves on the call. One young man said:

> Well, I started getting interested in Christianity when
> I played for a certain club, and the academy manager
> was called Simon. This was three years ago. Simon was
> a marvellous coach. But, more than that, he was an
> incredible guy. He had the highest professional standards
> for us and for himself. He oozed integrity. He was a great
> guy. Somebody said to me, 'He's a Christian, your coach.'
> I asked Simon about Jesus and he helped me to understand
> the Christian message, which has changed my life these
> past three years.

The following week, other people joined the Zoom call. There were twenty or thirty new boys introducing themselves to the group. You know what's coming, don't you? One young lad said, 'Well, five years ago, I was an apprentice at such-and-such a club, and the head of the academy was called Simon.' Same guy, same story, same vibrancy, same linking of the message of Jesus to the behaviour of the Christian. And I'm not exaggerating when I say that the following week it was a hat-trick!

The third week, a boy came to the call and a few of the others ask, 'How's Simon getting on?'

And I said, 'No way!'

Yes way! He was Simon's contact. This 25-year-old had come through the apprenticeship programme and met Christ because he thought the way Simon carried the gospel was attractive. Isn't it marvellous? In professional football, the little world I work in, people meet Christ because the gospel was taught to Simon, and he could not help but live with Christ at the centre. The impact on the world he works in goes on and people meet Christ.

So, what is our hope? Christ alone; the Christ who died for us and smashed death. The Christ who will return to own us on that final day. The Christ who lives in us right now. This is the gospel; this is the great hope and power that changes the life of a person who knows Christ personally and makes the gospel attractive.

> May I know your power to live, Lord? May your godliness
> flood through me. May the attraction of Jesus who lives
> in me reach people for himself and give me life today.
> May it be so, Lord.
> Amen.

Our Hope: The Glory of God! (Romans 5:1–5)

Jeremy McQuoid

Jeremy McQuoid is the Teaching Pastor at Deeside Christian Fellowship in Aberdeen and Chair of Keswick Ministries. He is a trustee of Pathways Scotland, a network that seeks to encourage a new generation into gospel ministry. Jeremy has written several books, including *The Amazing Cross* and devotional guides to Mark's Gospel and Hebrews. He is married to Elizabeth and they have three sons.

Several years ago, a submarine was rammed by a ship off the coast of Massachusetts in the United States. The submarine sank immediately and the entire crew was trapped for several days. No expense was spared to try to rescue the crew. Eventually, they sent a deep-sea diver down to see if he could help. The diver heard a tapping on the steel wall of the sunken sub, so he placed his helmet up against the side, to listen in. As he listened, he worked out that the crew were using Morse code, so he leaned in all the closer. They were tapping the words, again and again, 'Is there any hope? Is there any hope?' Sadly, in the end, although they recovered the submarine, all six men on board were lost.

That story is almost a symbol of the age in which we live. With all the uncertainty we face right now – with the Covid-19 pandemic and the fear it produces, with the political volatility of our world, the sexual confusion of our generation and the hopelessness of secularism – our culture today is tapping out that same question as the men in the submarine: 'Is there any hope? Is there any hope in our world?'

Paul's emphatic answer in Romans 5 is that there is a real, tangible hope. There is so much hope, in fact, that this passage is almost like a cascading waterfall of faith-filled facts that all lead to hope. Paul is saying here that, for the man or woman who is trusting in Jesus Christ, all roads lead to hope; for those staying close to Jesus Christ during this age of fear, all roads lead to hope. In Romans 5, Paul brings us this hope by reminding us of the basic facts of our salvation. He begins by saying that justification leads to hope, which is in verses 1–2 of the passage. Verse 1 begins with the word 'Therefore', and Paul is pointing back to the whole argument of Romans 1 – 4, which centres around this vital concept of justification.

Justification leads to hope

The word 'justification' means to be declared righteous. It is core to our salvation. In the previous chapter, Paul explained that justification goes right the way back to Abraham. You'll remember how God told the ageing Abraham to look up at the night sky and see if he could count the stars. God made him a promise that he would have children as numerous as the stars in the sky. If Abraham simply took God at his word, it would be 'credited to him as righteousness' – that's the key phrase (Genesis 15:6). In other words, Abraham did not have to impress God with good deeds to be in a right relationship with him. He would be in that right relationship if he simply believed God's amazing promises.

We find ourselves in a similar situation to Abraham. If we simply accept by faith God's amazing promise that Christ paid for our sin at the cross, and that he rose again to begin the new creation in our hearts, then God will credit us, he will credit our lives with the righteousness of Jesus Christ. We will enter what Martin Luther famously called 'the wonderful' or 'the joyful exchange':[1] we hand our sins over to Jesus Christ and we receive from him, freely, this gift called righteousness – a perfect record of righteousness. So, if you're a Christian, when God looks at your life right now, he can say of you what he said of Jesus at his baptism: 'This is My beloved Son, in whom I am well pleased' (Matthew 3:17 NKJV). That's what God says over you, today – 'This is my beloved son, this is my beloved daughter, in whom I am well pleased.' God is pleased with us because of Christ. We are declared righteous because of Jesus. That is justification, and justification is the bullseye of salvation.

Paul now moves on to consider the fruit of justification; how justification leads to a whole series of wonderful things ending in hope.

Peace

To begin with, Paul says, justification leads to peace with God: 'Since we have been justified through faith, we have peace with God through our Lord Jesus Christ' (Romans 5:1). In other words, our previous hostility towards our Creator is over now, and we enjoy that beautiful Hebrew concept, *shalom* with God. We have peace with God. The Hebrew word *shalom* is richer than the English word 'peace'. *Shalom* is not just the absence of war, it's a sense of total inner well-being. Even if we're in isolation, even if we're worried about our jobs, finances or elderly loved ones, we can still have this peace – this *shalom* – with God. Paul says it's a peace that passes understanding; it's not dependent on our circumstances. That's why Paul could sing hymns in a prison cell when he was in Philippi. In

Philippians 4, he says, 'present your requests to God. And the peace of God, which transcends all understanding, will guard your hearts and your minds in Christ Jesus' (Philippians 4:6–7). Brothers and sisters, if you are feeling troubled today, then tap into this peace with God. Whatever happens to you in this life (and a lot can happen), your soul is hidden with Christ in God.

Psalm 46 has been quoted a lot during this pandemic. Psalm 46 pictures complete disaster; it pictures the earth being removed and mountains falling into the sea. It presents the worst that could possibly happen. But, while the whole world is in uproar, the psalmist says, 'There is this river whose streams make glad the city of God' (Psalm 46:4). There is a constant serenity in God's presence that you and I can tap into. So, justification leads to peace with God.

Grace

It also leads to grace, says Paul. Romans 5:2: 'we have gained access by faith into this grace in which we now stand'. Notice, we *stand* in grace. Grace is a permanent foundation in our lives, like having our feet set in the concrete of God's goodness. God doesn't just save us by his grace and then move us on to performance-based contracts. No. We stand in grace every day. We are not God's employees, striving to be his sons and daughters. We are already his beloved sons and daughters, chosen before the world began, so we seek to please our heavenly Father out of thankfulness for the secure relationship that we already have with him. It's so important that we grasp this truth.

Paul uses the word 'striving' quite often to talk about the striving for holiness in our lives. There is real, Spirit-inspired striving in all of our lives but it's not a striving to gain God's favour. That's not what it's all about; we already have God's favour. It is a striving to please him from our settled position as sons and daughters of God. Even when we fall, we can come back to the cross in repentance, and God showers his grace on us all over again. We stand in grace today, and we will never spend another moment of our whole existence outside the orbit of God's grace, his unmerited favour towards us.

So, justification leads to peace with God, which leads to this grace in which we stand, which then leads to hope.

Hope

Verse 2 says, 'we boast in the hope of the glory of God'. God's glory will one day fill a new heaven and a new earth, and the sneering and the hostility that the name of Jesus provokes in the world today will give way, on that final day, to bended knees and worldwide worship. Habakkuk's prophecy will come true: 'the earth will be filled with the knowledge of the glory of the LORD, As the waters cover the sea' (Habakkuk 2:14 NKJV). Our hope today, as Christians, is the hope of the glory of God. The new creation which God is preparing for us – that new creation – will be wonderful. It will be breathtaking, but it will be wonderful because it will be lit up by the glory of God.

So, if you're a Christian today and you're looking forward only to your mansion in the sky, you are missing the whole point of the new creation. Psalm 84 says, 'How lovely is your dwelling-place, LORD Almighty! My soul . . . faints for the courts of the LORD' (Psalm 84:1–2). The new creation will be wonderful because God's glory will light it up. There will be no need for the sun, says John in Revelation, for the Lamb will light up the heavenly city. C. S. Lewis, speaking of longings for the new creation said, 'We do not want merely to see beauty, we want to be united with beauty, we want to pass into it and become part of it'.[2] Heaven will be heaven because we will be surrounded by the glory of God, which is so wonderful it will make every earthly pleasure seem like a passing shadow.

Paul is saying in this passage, justification leads to hope – the hope of the glory of God.

Suffering leads to hope

Paul goes on to say not only does justification lead to hope but even suffering leads to hope. We wouldn't expect suffering to lead to hope, would we? We think that suffering leads to disillusionment, but that is categorically not what Paul is saying here. Romans 5:3 says, 'Not only so, but we also glory' – there's that word again – 'we also glory in our sufferings'. There is something exultant about Paul's language here that just doesn't seem to match the theme of suffering. But Paul wants to convince us that suffering in the Christian life is not something to speak of in whispered tones as though it were a sign that God was disapproving of us. It is something to glory in, just as much as we revel in the glory of God. Notice here that Paul moves seamlessly from speaking of the glory of God and the new heavens and new earth, in verse 2, to the glory of suffering. But how can Paul possibly think like that?

We glory not because the suffering itself is pleasant. No suffering is pleasant at the time (see Hebrews 12:11). Paul is certainly not underestimating what suffering can do to our whole psyche. You remember, he lists his own sufferings in other passages: his shipwrecks, beatings and being left for dead (see, for example, 2 Corinthians 11:24). He also talks about his thorn in the flesh; he had prayed several times for God to remove that thorn but God said no (see 2 Corinthians 12:7–9). Paul has carried the scars of Christ on his body; he doesn't want to be glib about suffering. The truth is that God has written some of the worst scripts for some of his best people.

Paul says here that we glory in our sufferings because of what our sufferings produce. Romans 5:3–4 tell us, 'suffering produces perseverance; perseverance, character; and character, hope'. The end result of the suffering that God ordains, that he allows in our lives, is hope. So, we need to learn to view our suffering as Christians in a whole new way. Paul says to the Philippians, 'it has been granted to you [it has been given to you, like a gift] on behalf of Christ not only to believe in him, but also to suffer for him' (Philippians 1:29). Suffering chisels out per-severance and character – two wonderful traits that Christ will reward at the end of time. God achieves something in our lives through our suffering that he cannot achieve in any other way.

Some of you may know the story of Louis Braille. There is a little awl dedicated to him in the French Academy of Sciences (an awl is a sharp little instrument that is used for punching holes). When Louis Braille was only 9 years old, an awl fell on him and he lost the sight in one eye and then, eventually, in both eyes. The situation was so tragic that he had to be sent off to a special school by his parents. But that little awl is in the Academy of Sciences not just to remind us of the accident but also because, later on, Louis Braille used that same awl to develop the system of punching holes in paper that has helped millions of sight-impaired people around the world to read. That awl, which brought such suffering in Louis Braille's own life, led to a wonderful invention that has blessed millions of lives in a way that could never have been imagined when Braille was blinded as a child. The suffering wasn't wanted – of course it wasn't welcomed – it caused huge trauma in his life but it led to significant blessing that could not have occurred in any other way.

Brothers and sisters, God produces great things in our lives, often through the suffering that he sovereignly ordains for us. Charles Spurgeon, a nineteenth-century Baptist preacher, who suffered from depression for most of his life, said, 'Many men owe the grandeur of their lives to their tremendous difficulties'.[3] God wants us to view our suffering in a whole new way. Look at all the struggles in your life right now that you wish weren't there, that you pray to God to be released from. Now, start to pray:

> Lord, may these struggles, may these tears that I shed, may the difficulties that I face in my life lead me to develop the kind of perseverance and character that will make me just like Jesus on the last day.

Our hope is certain

So, Paul is saying here that justification leads to hope and even suffering leads to hope. He rounds off this passage by saying our hope is certain – that's what Romans 5:5 is all about. Verse 5 reads, 'And hope does not put us to shame.' In other words, we can be confident that our hope is certain. The reason we know that our hope is certain is, as the verse goes on, 'because God's love has been poured out into our hearts through the Holy Spirit, who has been given to us'. So, our subjective experience of the love of God today is a guarantee that our hope is not a pipe dream; that we will, one day, bask in God's love for ever.

Now, Paul is not talking here about an objective truth. All of the blessings he has mentioned so far are built on the objective truth of Christ's dying for us, as a historical event in the past. Justification is an objective reality; we have peace with God, whether we feel it today or not. There is a lot of objective truth in this passage. But this love of God has been poured into our hearts and it is something that we *feel*. It is subjective. Of course, any time we talk about feelings in the Christian life, it's a tricky business. Perhaps we are wary of talking about them: 'Let's just stick with the facts of the faith, not changeable, hard-to-quantify emotions.' But God wants us to feel his love in our souls today. He has poured his love into our hearts. It hasn't just been trickled in there, it has been poured like a waterfall by the Holy Spirit, who lives within us. It's one thing for each of us to say, 'I know that God loves me because Christ died for me two thousand years ago.' We could be thinking that and yet we are struggling to feel his love today. But God wants us to feel his love in our souls right now.

The Spirit's presence in our lives is an emotional thing, like David dancing for joy as he entered Jerusalem with the Ark of God. While we don't want to build our lives purely on experience (there is a danger, of course, in relying on pure emotionalism), God wants us to experience his love. Sometimes we think, as good evangelicals, that we honour God when we are constantly bowed down by our sins and our sense of unworthiness – that's a trait that I recognize in my own heart. We dare not be too joyful because that wouldn't reflect an appropriate sense of repentance. *But* misery doesn't honour God. This passage is jam-packed with truths that should set our hearts on fire. Don't dwell on sins that have been forgiven; dwell on the love that has forgiven them. This love is living in us now, all the time.

The Sky Sports channel has a strap line that says 'feel it all'. Have you ever seen that on the television? 'Feel it all.' Now that's just talking about the emotions of football, a game. Paul is talking here about eternal glory. While it's true that we cannot experience the full joy of salvation until that last day dawns, we can experience part of it here and now.

Dwell on the peace that you have with your Creator. Dwell on the joy of being a redeemed son or daughter of the King. Dwell on the daily presence of the Holy Spirit in your heart. Dwell on the glory that is coming: '"no eye has seen . . . no ear has heard . . . no . . . mind has conceived" – the things that God has prepared for those who love him' (1 Corinthians 2:9). When we get to Romans 8, Paul says,

> The Spirit himself testifies with our spirit that we are
> God's children. Now if we are children, then we are
> heirs – heirs of God and co-heirs with Christ, if indeed
> we share in his sufferings in order that we may also share
> in his glory.
> (Romans 8:16–17)

God's love is not something in the past tense. God's love is live now. God wants you to be fully satisfied with his love today, as you wait for that love to be fully unleashed in the world to come. Feel it all – that's what Paul's saying here – feel it all, until a new day dawns and the Morning Star rises in your heart.

All roads lead to hope for the Christian, that's what Paul is saying in this passage. Justification leads to hope, even suffering leads to hope, and our hope is absolutely certain.

May God's Spirit fill your heart with the hope of glory today.

Notes

1. Michael Reeves, *The Unquenchable Flame: Discovering the Heart of the Reformation* (B&H Publishing, 2010), p. 50.
2. C. S. Lewis, *The Weight of Glory* (William Collins, 2013), p. 42.
3. C. H. Spurgeon, *The Complete Works of Charles Spurgeon, Volume 86: The Sword and the Trowel, Volume 7* (Delmarva Publications, 2015), p. 420.

Keswick Resources

We are delighted to be able to make the great Bible teaching from Keswick available all year round. Our resources can be accessed from three websites in a number of ways.

Keswick Ministries
Virtually Keswick Convention
On our website, you can find audio catch-ups from the 2020 Convention. This teaching is free to access and download. Go to https://vkc.keswickministries.org and click on the Daily Programmes and Events pages. The talks are also featured on the Keswick Convention YouTube channel.

USB sticks containing all the teaching from Virtually Keswick Convention are available to purchase too.

Talks Library
Bible Readings, Evening Celebrations, Lectures and Seminars from the past 10 years of the Keswick Convention, including Virtually Keswick Convention, are free to access and download in mp3 format. Go to https://keswickministries.org/talks-library.

Podcasts

- *The Keswick Convention Podcast* brings you interviews with guests and speakers from the forthcoming Convention in the summer. Presented by James Cary, the show is a mix of testimony, theology and reflection.
- *Kes Talks Podcast* includes talks from God's Word, given over the past twenty-five years by a variety of speakers at the Keswick Convention. We pray that the talks will be particularly helpful to you at this time.

Both these podcasts are available on iTunes and Spotify, as well as on podcasting apps.

Essential Christian

On this site, you can access Keswick teaching from as far back as 1957! Bible Readings, Evening Celebrations, Seminars and Lectures are all available in various formats, including CD, DVD, mp3 and USB stick. There are also Keswick Live albums and albums by worship leaders and artists who have performed at Keswick, including Stuart Townend and Keith and Kristen Getty. Go to www. essentialchristian.com/keswick.

Clayton TV

Free online viewing of Keswick Bible Readings and Lectures is available at www.clayton.tv.

If you would like to give towards the provision of Keswick Ministries free resources, such as our podcasts and online talks or to our wider ministry, please go to www.keswickministries.org/donate. Thank you for your support.

Keswick Ministries

Our purpose

Keswick Ministries exists to inspire and equip Christians to love and live for Christ in his world.

God's purpose is to bring his blessing to all the nations of the world (Genesis 12:3). That promise of blessing, which touches every aspect of human life, is ultimately fulfilled through the life, death, resurrection, ascension and future return of Christ. All of the people of God are called to participate in his missionary purposes, wherever he may place them. The central vision of Keswick Ministries is to see the people of God equipped, inspired and refreshed to fulfil that calling, directed and guided by God's Word in the power of his Spirit, for the glory of his Son.

Our priorities

There are three fundamental priorities which shape all that we do as we look to serve the local church.

- **Hearing God's Word**
  The Scriptures are the foundation for the church's life, growth and mission, and Keswick Ministries is committed to preach and teach God's Word in a way that is faithful to Scripture and relevant to Christians of all ages and backgrounds.

- **Becoming like God's Son**
  From its earliest days, the Keswick movement has
  encouraged Christians to live godly lives in the power
  of the Spirit, to grow in Christlikeness and to live
  under his Lordship in every area of life. This is God's
  will for his people in every culture and generation.
- **Serving God's mission**
  The authentic response to God's Word is obedience
  to his mission, and the inevitable result of
  Christlikeness is sacrificial service. Keswick
  Ministries seeks to encourage committed
  discipleship in family life, work and society, and
  energetic engagement in the cause of world mission.

Our ministry

- **Keswick Convention**
  The Convention attracts some 15,000 Christians
  from the UK and around the world to Keswick
  every summer. It provides Bible teaching for all ages,
  vibrant worship, a sense of unity across generations
  and denominations, and an inspirational call to serve
  Christ in the world. It caters for children of all ages
  and has a strong youth and young adult programme.
  And it all takes place in the beautiful Lake District –
  a perfect setting for rest, recreation and refreshment.
- **Keswick fellowship**
  For more than 140 years, the work of Keswick has
  affected churches worldwide, not just through

individuals being changed but also through Bible conventions that originate or draw their inspiration from the Keswick Convention. Today, there is a network of events that share Keswick Ministries' priorities across the UK and in many parts of Europe, Asia, North America, Australia, Africa and the Caribbean. Keswick Ministries is committed to strengthen the network in the UK and beyond, through prayer, news and cooperative activity.

- **Keswick teaching and training**
  Keswick Ministries is developing a range of inspiring, equipping, Bible-centred teaching and training that focuses on 'whole-of-life' discipleship. This builds on the same concern that started the Convention, that all Christians live godly lives in the power of the Spirit in all spheres of life in God's world. Some of the events focus on equipping. They are smaller and more intensive. Others focus on inspiring. Some are for pastors, others for those in other forms of church leadership, while many are for any Christian. All courses aim to see participants return home refreshed to serve.

- **Keswick resources**
  Keswick Ministries produces a range of books, devotionals and study guides as well as digital resources to inspire and equip Christians to live for Christ. The printed resources focus on the core foundations of Christian life and mission, and help Christians in their walk with Christ. The digital

resources make teaching and sung worship from the Keswick Convention available in a variety of ways.

Our unity

The Keswick movement worldwide has adopted a key Pauline statement to describe its gospel inclusivity: 'All one in Christ Jesus' (Galatians 3:28). Keswick Ministries works with evangelicals from a wide variety of church backgrounds, on the understanding that they share a commitment to the essential truths of the Christian faith as set out in our statement of belief.

Our contact details

T: 017687 80075
E: info@keswickministries.org
W: www.keswickministries.org
Mail: Keswick Ministries, Rawnsley Centre, Main Street, Keswick, Cumbria, CA12 5NP, England

Keswick Ministries

HEARING · BECOMING · SERVING

KESWICK CONVENTION 2021

FAITHFUL

WEEK	**WEEK**	**WEEK**
ONE	**TWO**	**THREE**
17 - 23 July	24 - 30 July	31 July - 6 August

—— *Bible Readers* ——

🎙 **ALISTAIR BEGG**   🎙 **SIMON MANCHESTER**   🎙 **MIKE MEYNELL**

—— *Worship Leaders* ——

🎵 **COLIN WEBSTER PHIL MOORE**   🎵 **BEN SLEE**   🎵 **OLLY KNIGHT**

"The steadfast love of the LORD never ceases; his mercies never come to an end; they are new every morning; great is your faithfulness"

Lamentations 3:22-23

WWW.KESWICKMINISTRIES.ORG

f @KeswickConvention   🐦 @KeswickC   📞 017687 80275   @ info@keswickministries.org